The Money Chase

Angel Investors and Venture Capitalists

A Two Volume Set

The CEO Handbook - Volume Three

Dr. Earl R. Smith II

Raven Press
Copyright 2014

About This Book

———

The Money Chase has been the death of many good companies. There are a range of reasons why this is so. Some companies simply do not deserve funding - they are not an attractive investment opportunity. Others embark on the money chase too early. They haven't established the business base to justify funding. Still others are run by people who seem to like the money chase better than running the business. All of these reasons and more make embarking on the search for venture funding a perilous business which risks your company and all it may become.

This volume is divided into two parts. The first is focused on Angel Investors. These tend to be early-stage investors of high net worth who are investing their own funds. The second part is focused on venture capitalists. These are individuals who generally invest in later stage companies and who are investing funds raised from institutional sources.

My purpose in writing this book is to give you some sense of how to approach these two types of investors. I've tried to give you some insight into how they think and how they analyze opportunities for investment. It is my hope that you will come away from reading this book with a better understanding of how to approach investors, how to present to them and how to establish productive relationships with them after they have funded your company.

About Me

I am a serial entrepreneur, political and social theorist, published author and speaker. A veteran of Wall Street, I have served as CEO/Senior Partner for all of the companies which I founded. My experience includes designing and organizing companies, business/technology management, team building, strategic alliances, negotiating complex arrangements, governance & compliance, resourcing & financing, mergers & acquisitions, management/team/board assessment, coaching and strategic and tactical planning and implementation. I serve on boards of directors and advisory boards, as well as in interim senior management positions. My expertise includes innovation, governance, succession planning, mergers & acquisitions, team building, strategic planning, turnarounds and reorganization.

I have been mentoring senior executives and corporations for more than two decades. I got into mentoring after a successful career as a recidivist entrepreneur. I founded and built six companies. The experience of building those businesses brought many good times but I have recently been thinking about all those clients I mentored and the successes that they have had. Some of my fondest memories have resulted from those mentoring engagements.

Over the years, I have provided executive mentoring, leadership guidance, organizational support, team and life mentoring. Each is different but the focus has always been the same – working to help my clients unlock their potential and enjoy successes that they never thought possible.

I provide mentoring to those who have both the courage and determination to make a truly transformational journey. My approach is heavily influenced by core principles of Zen Buddhism. I don't offer quick fixes or follow the latest fads. If you are willing to make the long journey – if it's time for you to come to know the person you really are and can become – if you intend to finally find the path you should be following – if you want to start living life you were truly meant to live – then perhaps we should talk. Send me an e-mail and we'll arrange a time to chat.

Dr. Earl R. Smith II
Washington, DC
June 2014
DrSmith@Dr-Smith.com

Getting Funded

There is no challenge that a founder faces that is quite like that of arranging the financial resources necessary to allow a company to grow. Most meet this test initially by accessing person resources. Next comes friends, family, grants and bank financing. But the time comes when those resources are no longer adequate. Once the limits have been reached, founders often turn to the hunt for investors. The first stop on this journey is often angle investors - those high net worth individuals who invest in early-stage companies.

For most founders - particularly first time entrepreneurs - this experience is much like traveling to a foreign country in which both the language and customs are radically different. Much time and effort can be lost in trying to navigate the reefs and shoals of obtaining angel investment. Many companies don't make the journey out of early-stage simply because the founders don't understand those differences and how to effectively navigate through them.

The purpose of this book is to give you a glimpse into the world of the angel investor. If you can manage to see the world through the eyes of potential investors in your company, your chances of successfully arranging needed financial resources increases substantially.

Table of Contents

Angel Investors

Venture Capitalists

Angel Investors – Getting Funded

Introduction

I wrote this book to help CEOs better understand Angel Investors. Getting funded is one of the major challenges that they face. Without adequate financial resources, a company will be limited in what it can accomplish. The journey to funding is full of twists and turns - journeys into unfamiliar territories. CEOs are far more familiar with the business of their business than the world of the angel investor. But, if they are going to be successful in getting funded, they need to understand and accommodate the investor's objectives. More companies fail because of this challenge that should. In this book I will draw from my experience and tell you of the good and bad that angel investors can bring to your company. I'll give you a peek behind the curtain and let you in on their approaches to investment. My sincere hope is that, after reading this book, you will be better prepared for the journey and have a better chance of getting your company funded.

After a successful entrepreneurial career - I founded and built six companies and helped to launch two non-profit organizations - I took a break. Well, two breaks to be precise. The first took me to eastern Maryland. After leaving Manhattan - eighteen years in the big Apple - I wanted to take some time to slow down. I bought a farm, assembled a flock of sheep and trained Border Collies for five years. The flock got to about three hundred fifty head and I regularly wore out two braces of Collies each day - to their delight and mine. After five years, I sold the flock, farm and tractor (I still miss that tractor) and shipped the dogs to Scotland. I decided to pursue a PhD in political and social theory. Scotland seemed like the place - and the beer is better in the land of my ancestors. That took another four years and generated lots of wonderful experiences.

When the time came to return to the States, my wife and I opted for Washington, DC. There, so the theory went, I could pursue both interests. My love of political and social theory stayed with me and I found plenty of diversions. However, I found that my interests in entrepreneurial activity had changed - perhaps mellowed is a better word. The truth was that I no longer wanted to be the parent of a new company - being the grandparent seemed a more commodious role. I set about helping other CEOs build their businesses. That the experience was gratifying is pure understatement. I had always kept a finger or two in the teaching game but this was different. I could help others learn how to succeed and drastically steepen their learning curve.

At first, most of the people I worked with came to me through referrals from friends.

However, soon an increasing number of them came through investors - mostly angel investors - who had taken a stake in a company and were experiencing results that were somewhat less than acceptable. Now three out of four companies that I work with come through angel investors.

My experience working with these companies, their CEOs and the investors who brought me in has taught me a series of important lesions about how to and how not to approach the process of investing in early-stage companies. I decided to put some of those lessons into an article and sent it out for comment. The responses were striking. Many accused me of highlighting their own mistakes - or worse, accused me of telling their story to the world. Most asked how to improve results. *Angel Investing - Improving Results* is a response to those requests. It is a handbook for angel investors. They can use it to master - or just plain avoid - some of the most difficult challenges - the ones that can turn investments into write-offs.

Nothing in this book is a criticism of any particular person or group. The experiences that it draws upon come from working with dozens of companies and investors. The difficulty in writing a book about common mistakes is that, if it is to be useful, it needs to focus on the human tendencies that lead to those mistakes. Writing about human foibles - messes that we all step in from time to time - can easily seem a criticism rather unconstructive. That is not my intent here. A writing mentor of mine was fond of saying "*if you are going to write about something, make sure that that something is real*". As I subsequently discovered, writing about the real means writing about real people.

That brings me to the final comment I want to offer before getting down to the meat of the subject. I am indebted beyond saying to those angel investors that I have worked with. Their willingness to talk openly about their mistakes - the opportunities foregone - as well as their successes - has made this book possible. Without that, I would just be writing fictional accounts of a process that I viewed from a non-investor perspective. I dedicate this book to all of them. I am certain that they share my hope that it leads to improved results and happier times for all angels. They are, after all, angels

.

Red-Teaming: Improve Your Chances of Getting Funded

This is a proven method for improving the chances of success. Not rocket science – nothing very difficult – just a straightforward and logical approach to a recurring challenge. If you are out to win – this has to be one of the tools in your toolbox.

~~~~~~~~~~~~~~~~~~~~

The beginnings of a good idea

Recently I sat in on a presentation that two founders of a technology start-up made to a front-line venture capitalist. What was most striking about the experience was that, from one point of view, the founders seemed very well prepared. Their presentation was polished and contained all the usual sections, their slide show was professional quality, and they spoke with passion and deep knowledge about their space. The materials which they provided were all neatly and professionally packaged.

But early in the meeting it became apparent that the team was not prepared for what they were encountering. Their pitch was clearly more appropriate for a group of fellow technologists. They had not taken into consideration the predictable concerns and perspective of the person to whom they were presenting. The VC had interrupted the flow of their pitch with a couple of completely normal threshold questions and it went downhill from there.

After the session I asked the investor how frequently this kind of thing happens. He shook his head and responded "More often than I would like and far more often than needs be. The tragedy is that it doesn't have to." When I asked what he meant he replied "I'm probably the first outsider that they have ever given this presentation to. As a result their pitch comes to me without any real critical review. But what is most discouraging is that their entire presentation was not focused on my concerns as an investor but on a 'preaching to the choir' gathering of their peers. And what they don't seem to realize is that mine is a very tight community and we talk to each other on a regular basis. What these guys did today was not only establish a negative brand with me but with any others that I end up talking to about them."

I immediately understood what he meant. One of the services I provide to clients is the establishment of an advisory board designed as a high level, business development engine. I had built such a board for a company that is in the enterprise level software business. One of the company's proudest achievements was that they had earned a high level of certification for their software development process. This certification was prominently mentioned in all of their promotional materials and on their website.

The senior management team was presenting during the first ever gathering of the board. The advisory board consisted of five very high-level individuals with an average of three to four decades of experience. Most had built businesses or run very large organizations. All of them had risen to the top of their profession. This first meeting was designed to bring the board members up to speed.

The software certification was prominently displayed on one of the earliest slides that the chief operating officer presented. One of the board members interrupted the pitch with a question, "OK, I'm one of your customers. Other than making your software more expensive, what is the value of this certification to me?" It quickly became clear that any answer which the team could offer was focused on the 'choir' – those individuals who had already bought in to the value of the certification process. They were not able to provide an answer from a client's perspective. As a result, they lost the confidence of the board and had to work hard to get it back.

As I related the story my friend nodded and ruefully smiled. "I'm glad to see that this happens to other people. I had taken to thinking that mine was the only profession that encountered this kind of thing."

As we talked and told war stories, a conversation with a former partner in the movie business came back to mind. Sy had been talking about how much more difficult it was for new talent to get experience since the demise of a vast network of performance venues that used to serve as incubators. Again, there was the pattern. People need a space where they can knock off the rough edges and focus their presentation.

What came out of this was a vision for a kind of 'presentation boot camp' – a space where founders could refine and focus their pitch without incurring the liability of having to learn under fire – and avoid establishing a negative branding in front of potential investors to boot.

Borrowing from another space

I first came across the idea of red-teaming years and years ago when I was working in the government contracting space. I subsequently learned that it is also widely used in the commercial sector. A proposal team will subject the results of its efforts to a panel of outside experts well prior to submission to the client. The process is designed to make sure 1) that the proposal correctly addresses the RFP; 2) that the solutions offered are ones that would likely be accepted by the client; 3) that the costing of the proposal has been done correctly and does not contain any extraneous expenditures and 4) that the team can present and defend the proposal in a highly professional and effective manner.

This process is standard procedure – in fact, widely considered an essential part of best practices – in the government contracting space. The danger of not following these best practices is severe. I know companies which, in the re-bidding process, failed to adequately challenge the proposal team and lost contracts that they should have won.

When you prepare a presentation for funding you run the considerable risk of becoming so close to the trees that you grow less and less capable of assessing the forest. A professional, independent review of your funding request, well before you present it to the first VC, could make the difference between being funded or wasting a lot of time – yours and the VC's. With our knowledge of the investor's decision making process and wide range of contacts within the VC and private equity communities, I can organize and facilitate a red team review that can significantly improve your chances of being funded.

Red teaming can be applied with considerable benefit to testing and refining presentations to venture capitalists. This process can assure that it meets the needs; adequately address is the concerns; is clearly and professionally delivered and definitively answers the threshold questions that the investor is likely to have.

Red Teaming a Request for Funding

The best way (in fact, the only reliable way) to make sure your presentation is well focused and provides what a VC requires is to have it reviewed by an objective panel that sees it through the eyes of a potential investor. A red team looks at the presentation exactly that way. They evaluate the request for funding, projected use of proceeds, business plan, value proposition and management team as if they are being asked to invest in the company; looking for weaknesses and strengths and checking to make sure threshold questions are addressed in a way which will lead to the next level of discussions.

A red team review is arguably the most important step in the entire cycle of preparing for and delivering a presentation to potential investors. I have developed an approach which will improve chances for getting funded. The core of the process is a group of people who will evaluate your request for funding, and your company, from the investor's perspective.

Red team members read your materials as if they were evaluating you for funding. This means that they will not be advocates for your company. Quite the opposite – if your presentation has serious problems or if they don't get what you're trying to say, it will more likely be, "This is not making sense as an investment!"

That in itself is more than a lot of VCs will do. They are in the business of finding opportunities and making investments – not critiquing your presentation. Many times all you will get is "Thanks for coming in – we will get back to you if we are interested." But a red team goes the extra step – it is in the business of helping you improve your chances of getting funded. In that role they play hardball; team members can be very critical, step on your toes if necessary, and pull no punches. A red team member who holds back honest and incisive criticism because of a fear of hurting someone's feelings is not helping the effort.

Red teaming can be a very unsettling experience for some founders – but the goal of each and every member of the team is to help improve the presentation, value proposition, business plan and chances of getting funded. Remember, to make a success you occasionally have to break a few egos!

Here are some guidelines we follow for forming and running a red team review:

- Because of their experience, members of our red teams emulate the process and mindset of the VCs that the company is going to present to.

- We pick at least three people to serve on each team.
- They are knowledgeable in the company's space.
- Team members must have no prior connection with the company that is presenting.
- They must be willing and able to commit the necessary time and attention to the process.
- We insist that members are given at least two days to read the materials to be used in the presentation and do a bit of personal research.
- Team members must be committed to helping the founders improve their chances of getting funded.

Benefits of a Red Team Review

Our independent review procedure emulates the investor community's initial-review decision making. We simulate first meetings with VCs and critically review the presentations. Our process delivers an in-depth, interactive debriefing of a funding request. The results will provide you with guidance and direction on what must be done to improve your probability of being funded.

Red team members read and research materials and discuss them among themselves prior to your actual presentation.

The team then sits through your presentation – a simulated initial meeting with a potential investor. The focus of the evaluation is on how well you presented your business plan, value proposition and answered the threshold questions that an investor is likely to ask.

Finally, the team delivers a thoroughly interactive debriefing. The focus is on specific recommendations for resolution of major issues. They also present recommendations and guidance on improvements relative to strengths, weaknesses, opportunities and threats.

Red-Teaming Programs

My red teaming programs are designed to:

- Help founders become familiar with the process of red-teaming,
- Take them through a simulated initial meeting with a potential investor,
- Provide a critical review and assistance in refocusing and refining their presentation, and
- Guide them through the process of presenting to appropriate venture capitalists and private equity fund managers.

If you want to learn more about my red

teaming programs and how they can help
you improve your chances of getting
funded, send me an e-mail and we will
arrange a time for a free consultation.

Angel's Sins

In this case, I am talking about early-stage investors and the sins that they sometimes commit when they decide to back a start-up company. I spend a lot of time engaged with such companies - and much of that time working to set right sins that were committed when the first round of angel funding occurred. What follows is a partial list of 'sins' and a few suggestions that might both mitigate their impact and improve the investors' results.

CEO Compensation: I regularly come across pre-revenue companies that are paying CEOs at levels that would be prudent if the company was generating a run-rate in the twenty to thirty million-dollar ranges. As a result, lots of the investment capital is going out the door in the form of fat monthly checks. CEO compensation should reflect the condition of the company and the unavoidable fact that, in start-up situations, cash is a very rarest of commodities and needs conserving.

Top-Heavy Teams: I recently surveyed at a company that had a senior team that was appropriate for a much larger company. There was lots of talent available but they were underutilized. In this case, they had a fully competent director of human resources and an experienced vice president of finance. Both were high quality and very experienced people - not to mention very high cost. What the company really needed was a first-class recruiter and a competent bookkeeper. The team has to match the needs and current condition of the company. Sure, some amount of forward investing is appropriate but, when excessive; it can sink a company quickly.

Compensation Schemes: Quite often, I encounter companies that have compensation schemes that are not conditional on performance. These arrangements act as a disincentive and do not reflect the 'risk profile' of the company. A better way forward is to divide senior team base compensation into two categories - one for filling the role and a second based on results. A good measure of the prudence of a compensation plan for a start-up is the percentage of investment capital that goes to senior team members no matter what the results are - the smaller this percentage the better.

Technology Centric Focus: Many angel investors 'fall in love' with the technology and ignore the fact that even in the early stages the business of business is just as important as the business of the business. An unavoidable fact about any business is that implementation - not technology - is what makes the difference between success and failure. Certainly, the team needs a strong component of technologists. However, they only offer the possibility that the company will be a success.

Implementers - those driven to turn technology into revenues and profits, dominate winning teams - these people can build a successful company.

Hands-Off Oversight: Many investors seem to take the position that, once invested, the future of the company is up to the management team. Many of them actually sit on the board of the company but take passive roles. A key to start-up success is board oversight or 'adult supervision'. Without it, the effort can descend into a simple roll of the dice. Investors - or better, their professional representatives on the board - should play an active and forceful role in determining the strategic direction of the company. One of the strengths of many angel investors is that they have had successful careers - experience in building and managing businesses - and that experience is invaluable to a new company and team.

Fanciful Projections and Slide Stacks: The two most insidious - nay, dangerous - pieces of software for start-ups are Power Point and Excel. Both promote shallow thinking. Start-ups are particularly vulnerable to the kind of loose thinking and untested assumptions that spreadsheets and slide stacks seem to cultivate. I often encounter start-up companies that are using incredibly convoluted financial models - companies that have yet to put two months of cash-flow positive results on the books. This kind of over-engineering distracts from the simple fact that the company has yet to become a going concern. Most often focus on these Rube Goldberg models results in a continual re-setting of expectations and little change in the culture, focus or profitability of the company.

Performance Reviews: In going concerns, the performance reviews are a key to evaluating management. The board of directors uses the reviews to decide whether the company has the right CEO and senior team members. It is rare that I encounter a start-up that has this process in place - and rarer still to find formal reviews as part of the corporate records. Every member of a start-up team should be performance reviewed by the board on a regular basis. Those reviews should set compensation, initiate renegotiation contracts and arrange for severance when necessary.

Avoiding Sinning

In the start-up world, one in ten companies makes it to their fifth anniversary. My experience has been that most that fail do so because the team has performed poorly in the business of business - in other words, they do not fail because their value proposition - or the technology the heart of that value proposition - is faulty. They fail because they have not implemented the strategic and tactical vision in a way that generates revenue and an expanding customer base. Angel investors have it in their power to improve the odds. However, to do so requires a more focused and professional approach.

When I work with companies, one of my early statements is "there are no passengers in this boat - everybody gets an oar - and everybody gets assessed on how well or poorly they pull on that oar. For the boat to go straight and fast, hard and balanced pressure from all oars is the ticket. If one of you lets the team down, the boat will travel in circles. Now, stop talking about rowing and get to the oars." I have delivered this message any number of times with much the same effects. First, those who see themselves as passengers leave the team. (One CEO actually quit after a single one-hour session - went from our meeting to see the principal investor and was dismissed on the spot) These departures are very good things. I call it clearing out the deadwood.

Angel investors can adopt this more pro-active approach. The beginnings are in the relationship among their fellow investors. In team play, members learn quickly that telling their team members what they already know is not insulting - it is reinforcing. Angel investors can learn from this very wise practice. They can act as coaches or involve professional coaches. In this role, they can insist on a focused agenda and highly productive effort from all team members. But they can also work to support each other.

In most situations, a lead investor or partner will be advocating a particular company and investment strategy. Using this chapter as a template for challenging that partner can significantly reduce the possibility that failure will be the result. This process must have teeth and a dedication to finding the truth. Facile answers need to be challenged directly. Giving a gratuitous pass is no benefit to the person about to make an investment. The 'hot seat' needs to be hot rather than tepid.

If 'real friends don't let friends drive drunk', then real investors don't let other investors invest as if they were drunk. I recommend a variation of the concept of 'red-teaming'. The proponent of an investment should be 'forced' to respond to the following questions:

Are you over-compensating the CEO? What percentage of that compensation is contingent on performance? Why do you need all these people on the team? This is a start-up after all. Are you over-spending and underutilizing? What part of the compensation scheme for the team is contingent on performance? Why is that percentage so high? Are you the only one taking a risk here?

Yeah, the technology is 'neat' but what about the ability of the team to build a business? Have any of them actually done that? What makes you thin that this is anything but a 'science project'?

How involved are you or your professional representative going to be in determining the strategic direction of the company? Are you figuring on turning over the funds and embarking on another one of your 'round-the-world' treks? If so, you should probably kiss the money goodbye before your leave.

We looked at this slide stack and impressive spreadsheet and don't believe any of it. What makes you think that they can hit these targets, maintain these margins or manage this rate of growth? What happens to them if they don't? What are they risking if they don't?

Where are the baseline performance reviews on members of the senior team? We want to read your assessments and compare them against future results.

I have facilitated processes such as the one outlined above. The results have been dramatic. It is amazing how much better results become when the business of investing comes to be seen as a business.

Angel Investors to Avoid

I want to state at the very beginning that most angel investors I have worked with do not fall into the categories that follow. For the most part, they are honest, professional and dedicated to helping their portfolio companies thrive. To the extent that they have foibles, they are no better or worse than the rest of us. This article is about that small percentage of angel investors that can really give you heartburn and seriously damage your chances of building a successful business. Here are some of the types that you should avoid.

The Shadow CEO: The Shadow CEO is often a retired executive who has had significant success in the past. Some of them have run very large organizations successfully and retired with fat separation packages that they are using to fund their activities as an angel investor. To be clear, I have seen such people act very effectively as angel investors. But there are a small percentage of them that are control freaks. Their tendency is to invest with inexperienced or weak CEOs and manipulate them much as a puppeteer would. They pull the strings and, at critical moments, assert their dominance. The basic problem with this type is that they never allow the CEO or management team to grow. The team is always 'my kids' and dominated by the Shadow CEO. One characteristic of the portfolio companies of this type us that they tend to stay small and have limited success. Quite often, they simply limp along until the Shadow CEO loses interest and stops funding the company. One particularly insidious characteristic of the Shadow CEO is that, in the end, it is all about them. If the CEO or team begins to get too much of the limelight, they are likely to slap them down and reassert their dominance.

The Crazy, Rich Uncle: These are the toughest angel investors to walk away from. One of the reasons is that they are generally so accommodating and easy to get along with. A good early indication that you are dealing with a Crazy, Rich Uncle is the almost total lack of insistence on any performance metrics for you or your team. At first the freedom from performance metrics might feel pretty good, but the long term effect is that it is much harder to get your team to perform at its best. The reason is that their performance is not a factor in the continuing funding decisions made by the Crazy, Rich Uncle. There are some dark sides to this type through. Many of them are micro-managers and want to constantly second guess your smallest decisions. They might style themselves as a 'mentor' but their real intention is control much like the Shadow CEO. Their 'mentoring' can absorb substantial chunks of your time and energy. A second type of Crazy, Rich Uncle is the has-been who is seeking to relive their early life successes through the next generation. I call these the 'Little League Dads and Moms'. They treat their portfolio companies and the management teams as their children who they are molding in their own image. Well, I suspect you can see where that will lead you.

The Gaggle: One of the most significant trends in angel investing has been the professionalization of the groups of angel investors. Most of them have adopted policies and procedures that are common with the larger and later-stage venture capital funds. Some of the most effective and successful angel investors are part of these groups. But there are still echoes of the past to be found here and there. Successful angel investors are prudent, disciplined and professionally organized. The Gaggle is completely the opposite. They seem to fly by the seat of their pants and make decisions based more on emotion and gut feel. This is the source of one of their principal weaknesses. They are often committed today and looking for a way out tomorrow. A good indicator of The Gaggle is a very unstructured and unprofessional decision and diligence process. This signals a lack of seriousness and business savvy. They generally give themselves away through the questions that they ask. Most are superficial and are not followed up with deeper probing. A Gaggle will often waste your time and energy with an extended diligence process that ends up with them deciding not to invest. For many of these groups, this is their social time and you are their entertainment for the evening. Look out for loosely drawn 'investment criteria and policies' as they are a clear indicator that you are dealing with a Gaggle.

The Bottom Feeders: Bottom Feeders are predatory from the very beginning. Their real focus is on control of the intellectual property (IP) that you have or are developing. Often they will supply just enough funding to support the development of the IP and little or none for the monetization of the value proposition. The reason is that any monetization will work against their primary goal. Their goal is not to try to help your company grow; instead they make their money through intimidation, threats and lawsuits and eventual control of the IP. Bottom Feeders know you do not have the resources to fight them; mostly because they are controlling the resources you have. They know you will have to settle and, most likely, meet their demands. One of the best indicators of a Bottom Feeder is a history of bringing lawsuits against the principals of their portfolio companies. As a matter of course, it is prudent to do a search of the court records in the jurisdictions that the investor's portfolio companies operate. A bloom of suits will be a good indicator that you are dealing with a Bottom Feeder.

The Lead Broker: This is a particularly insidious type. The Lead Broker often puts themselves forward as a wealthy investor looking for good companies. Their initial pitch may be focused on their own ability to provide investment funds. But, as your conversations continue, the emphasis shifts. One form of Lead Broker will end up asking for a retainer. Once they have demonstrated some enthusiasm for your company, they suggest that the funding requirements exceed their capabilities. But not to worry; they will fill the need in return for a monthly retainer and success fee. They often promise to put their own money in along with their 'friends' investment. I have known Lead Brokers who regularly put in as little as ten percent of the total funding but try to keep themselves in a central position on the board of directors or as spokesman for the investor group. The truth is that you do not need these guys. If your company is investment quality, take it directly to the angel investor groups in your area and avoid the overhead.

The good news is that there are a lot of highly professional angel investors around. They do not fall into any of the above categories and consistently bring real value to their portfolio companies. One very useful rule is to avoid individual investors where possible and gravitate towards those highly professional groups of angels. It is often very easy to identify them. Most of these groups have websites which describe their interests, investment policies and portfolio companies. This makes your diligence much easier. If you focus on credible, professional investor groups, your chances of developing a productive relationship with a source of funding goes up considerably. Remember to push your diligence beyond the investor group. Good angel investors, once they have decided that they have an interest in investing in your company, will always facilitate your diligence. Most professional groups will be glad to introduce you to the senior management of their portfolio companies. This is your chance to find out what it is like to deal with the investment group from people who have first-hand experience.

Angel Investors – The Good, Bad and Very Ugly

There is a tendency among entrepreneurs to chase money wherever they find it. The pressure to find the financial resources so necessary to build a business can be over-mastering. Most of the time the partnerships which form between founders and angel investors are productive but, in a few cases, I have seen it turn very destructive. Companies that should have realized success have been held back by investor partnerships that have severely limited their potential or, in some cases, doomed them to failure.

Look Beyond the Checkbook

It may be hard to be discriminating when you are in the heat of the 'money hunt' but the sins of omission you commit while chasing investors can return ten-fold to destroy any chance of success. The problem become acute because of the incredible range of circumstances, experience and interests that angel investors bring to the table. Their having money to invest in not enough. You need to understand their basic motivations and what is driving them to act as an angel investor. You also need to understand that all investment money is not the same. Some money will help you succeed while other investments will be a poisoned pill that will reduce your chances of building the business you envision. Here are some 'sacred cows' that you need to slaughter:

Angel investors are in it for a return on their investment: Well, how can you argue with that? You would assume that the primary driver is always a return on investment. But, as you will read further on, that is not always the case. I know angel investors who are simply bored and looking for something to do and others who are frustrated CEO-wannabees. For some investors, it is all about a return but for others the return is secondary. You need to sort these two groups out. Do not listen just to what they say; it is what they do that is important.

They have money they; must be smart: This is another fallacy. Some of the dumbest and most self-destructive people I have ever met are wealthy. I have found only a weak correlation between wealth and intelligence and a slimmer one between wealth and wisdom. Many a destructive hubris has been built on a fat bank account. Investors have an important role in start-ups but pretense, omnipotence or omniscience can warp an investor's understanding of that role. Smart investors play their part in a highly professional and constructive manner. Seek them out; they are most likely the winners you want to associate with.

They have been successful in business so

they will know how we can be: Past success is not always a good indicator of wisdom going forward. In fact, great success can be counter-productive when they decide to work with start-up companies. I know one investor who continually regales his CEOs with stories of how he ran his company. Of course, the company was running over one hundred million annually when these stories took place. The CEOs, wanting to emulate his success, take steps that are entirely premature. The result is wasted resources and a dysfunctional corporate culture. Past business success is not a good indicator of professional performance as an investor. Remember, you are seeking an investor, not a shadow CEO.

They will become my close personal friends and advisers: Not a good idea; the correct focus of investors should produce a tension in the relationship with management. If you want a friend, buy a dog.

The Bad and the Very Ugly

The problem with writing about angel investors is that they come in an amazing variety. I have met lots of them and there is always something different about each. The ease of entry into the field may have something to do with it. The only real entry requirement is wealth beyond current needs. That's all it takes to become an angel investor. There are no educational requirements, courses to take or certifications to merit. Only a bank account and a decision to 'invest' are required to hang out a shingle and open up for business. Watch out for the following:

The Shadow CEO: I have met investors who purposefully pick weak or inexperienced CEOs to work with. Their real agenda is to run your company from the back seat. These investors are very intrusive and will push you to make decisions and commit resources that will put your company at risk. They are mostly successful entrepreneurs who have built and sold a business. In the process, they have lost touch with the necessary energy levels and passion that is essential to building a start-up into a going business. Mostly they remember the later stages of their company and the extended staff they had. Then they turn the CEO into a kind of executive assistant and attempt to run the company by proxy. Most of the companies in the portfolio of this type of investor remain very small. They generally have very complex Excel spreadsheet projections and poor records in meeting them. Stay away from the Shadow CEO; they are very dangerous investors.

The Crazy, Rich Uncle: This is probably the most dangerous type of angel investor because they are so easy on the management team. They are mostly retired and living comfortably. Their mission in life is to 'give back to the younger generation'. A clear indication of this type is the total lack of performance metrics and a weak statement of expectations. They can be very seductive to entrepreneurs but there is a dark side. Without stiff set of performance metrics, the company can develop a culture of permissiveness. That will feel good until the money runs out. A key indicator of this type is the feeling that the amounts of money involved are, at least initially, not sufficient to cause them concern. The expenditure patterns are not carefully monitored and discussions do not turn serious until the money is spent and the wolves are at the door. As an entrepreneur, you need to seek out investors who will be hard on you; insisting on strict performance metrics and precise definitions of roles. Take the easy way out and you will be in for a ride to nowhere with a crazy, rich uncle. Sure you will enjoy the ride but, in the end, you will be let off the bus in the middle of nowhere with a tarnished reputation for failure.

The Gaggle: Remember the old saying about a camel being a horse designed by a committee? These gaggles are fond of that kind of engagement. The investments that they make are very often selected in a very casual way and supervised fairly loosely. The problem comes as the group itself is very loosely organized. Different participants might have significantly different understandings of what it mean to be an investor and what that status entitles them to. The can range from complete indifference to total immersion in the management of the company. This situation can result in lots of pulling and pushing of the management team without an overarching strategic vision. Investments should be made based on clear and concise understandings codified in a detailed investment agreement.

The Bottom Feeders: You will meet some investors who are really only interested in your intellectual property. They 'drag the bottom' of the entrepreneurial community looking for weak teams with good ideas. Mostly they insist that their funding be used to develop the technology rather than developing revenues. Once the money runs out, they regretfully inform management that they are closing the company down and talking the intellectual property as compensation for their investment.

The Lead Broker: I have seen these lead brokers promote themselves into central roles in companies without putting much of any of their own money on the line. The net result is that the bulk of the investor group gets involved without much direct knowledge of the business or the management team. In one case, such a broker put together an investment in excess of one million dollars without making any investment of his own. He still managed a seat on the board and a dominate role in the management of the company. Be particularly careful of the broker who can invest but does not. This situation can turn nasty if expectations are not met. Finger pointing and recriminations can come to dominate the relationships among the investors. This could seriously damage chances of follow-on investments by the group.

The Good

Good angel investors always take a highly professional approach to the process and their portfolio companies. They generally focus in industries that they are familiar with. It is a good idea to avoid angel investors whose portfolio companies do not fit a close pattern. The best angel investors will often forgo the option of claiming a board seat and, instead, insist that an independent board member with professional experience be appointed. Beware of investors who seem to see investment in your company as an opportunity to enhance their reputation by sitting on yet another board. Here are some positive things to look for:

Success Breeds Success: There are angel investors who have the knack to help their portfolio companies thrive; while others seem to doom them to failure or stagnation. I know of one angel who specializes in little deals and has a well-developed ability to keep them that way.

Other investors seem to have the opposite skill. Their companies grow and prosper. It is a good idea to do some diligence on the track record of the investor. Go with the successful ones even if the deal terms are less generous.

The Investment Agreement: There ought to be a detailed investment agreement agreed to before any funds are transferred. This agreement should be very specific when it comes to the roles and responsibilities of each party. The best agreements provide for an earn-in by management based on performance. It also sets the ground rules for further investment. Good angel investors will require this as a matter of course. The worst ones will simply require a term sheet and then write a check. Remember that the absence of planning is the road to failure. Think of the investment agreement as a strategic plan for the relationship.

Strategic Agreement on Roles and Responsibilities: Good angel investors will insist that the roles and responsibilities for each party be very well understood from the very beginning. These roles will be codified in the investment agreement and specify the actions that each party will be able to take under a range of possible outcomes. Although such an agreement can complicate initial negotiations, it will help greatly when performance does not meet expectations and realignment become necessary.

Use of Proceeds: I have seen investors write rather large checks without insisting that there be an agreed upon use of proceeds. You can imagine what happened then. Entrepreneurs initially like the freedom to simply take the money and spend it as they see fit. But, more often than not, this leads to waste and spending on things that do not connect directly to the success of the company. One company, upon receiving funds in this way, spent a lot of the money on new laptops and cell phones with expensive service plans. They replaced very serviceable units. Another CEO kept paying his salary, even though results fell far below projections, and failed to pay suppliers. The result was a law suit that is almost certain to shut down the company. It is good business practice for the angel investors to insist on a detailed use of proceeds and for control over the spending of their money.

Insistence on Performance Metrics: As a CEO you should be insisting on performance metrics for every member of your team. That is just good management. Your investors should take the same approach. It may seem initially easier to deal with angel investors who are very lax about this, but it is far from best practices. I am not just talking about Excel spreadsheet metrics. They have to be much more detailed than that. Good performance metrics detail the responsibilities of each member of the management team and the way their performance will be measured. Everybody from the CEO to the receptionist should have a job description with metrics attached. And the metrics should be sufficiently detailed to drive evaluations based on performance. Performance should be the driver in determining both compensation and earned-in interest in the company. Performance metrics are a sign of a professional and productive organization. Start-ups with that culture have a much higher chance of success.

Focus on Governance Issues and Oversight: "Who's minding the store?" If the answer to that question is "nobody but us entrepreneurs", consider that a red flag. In the short-term, it may feel good to be free from oversight but, in the long-term, you are guaranteed to make more mistakes and waste more opportunities. The board of directors has a very important role to fill in any corporate structure and it is not just making sure that the investors get to a liquidity event as soon as possible. Good governance means overseeing the strategic planning process, dealing with issues of succession, audit and compensation, and providing for the protections and expansion of shareholder value. This fiduciary relationship with the shareholders is an important part of the corporate structure. Without it, management is under no effective supervision and the investment looks more like a roll of the dice than an investment.

Keep This In Mind: An angel investment creates a relationship that will help determine how successful you are going to be. Your skill in crafting that relationship is a test of how dedicated you are to the success of your company and team. If you take the easy way out, your chances of success will drop significantly. If you opt for the limp relationship with an inattentive investor, your prospects will suffer. Angel investors, the good ones, bring much more than money to the table. The good ones have helped their companies succeed and will help you do the same.

An Imbalance of Power

I often am asked by investors to 'take a look' at a company they have invested in. Generally, the request comes rather late in the game and after the current management has stretched - or, sometimes more properly, dissipated - the investment. These engagements produce recommendations that tend to be unsatisfying to all parties. It was after one particularly melancholy report that I began to look for the roots of the problem - tried to figure out why so many investments met the same unsatisfactory end.

Sure, there were the easy options - the usual suspects as they say. The value proposition was inadequate - management was not up to implementing - they were ahead of their time - or behind it. Experienced angel investors have heard - and sometimes offered - these and many more. However, none seemed edifying and as Gabriel Meurier observed, "*He who excuses himself, accuses himself*".

Business is, above all, a process of meeting and overcoming challenges. To say that the patient has died is sufficient if the objective is writing an obituary. However, I was so often called to the side of terminally ill, but still living, patients. Certainly, I wanted to figure out why obituaries seemed to become necessary so frequently but that was a smaller problem. A post-mortem is just that and of little help unless it can shed light on the fundamental cause - can point to a different approach to the process - one that might improve results. The main question was 'why does the fatal disease seem to set in in the first place'?

The point here is a variation on Albert Einstein's famous definition of insanity - "doing the same thing over and over with ever the expectation of different results". I set aside the usual suspects and began to ask myself 'what is it about the process that seems to generate unacceptable results so frequently?' The problem, after all, seemed endemic to angel investing.

While pressing this question, I was invited by a venture capitalist to review a set of portfolio of companies. I discovered that most of them shared the characteristics described above. Most were towards the end of a journey that began with much fanfare and hope. Most had burned through a great deal of investment without generating significant positive results. Most were so far into the pit that nothing much could be done for them without essentially sending much more good money after bad.

It was at this point that I came to realize that there was something about the process of investing that seemed to drive the basic numbers - seemed to almost guarantee that only one in ten start-ups would make it to their fifth anniversary without being put on life support. Something about the process forced investors to hope for that ten-times or twenty-times score - a score that would recoup their investment in the other nine and give them a net profit.

What was it about investing that seemed to produce so much loss? What forced investors to hold to this hope for a big score and accept the losses as inevitable?

When I put these questions to investors, I most often received tight variations on the same reply. *"It's just the way the game works?"* *"Investing is about risk and risk often leads to loss"*. I was tempted to accept 'reality' when, during a meeting with two investors about an engagement with one of their portfolio companies, I asked a question that opened the door to another possibility. The question was simple in form. The answer I received was profound far beyond expectations. Here is what I asked:

"Who is the client in this engagement?"

The immediate response was *"The Company, of course"*.

Now remember that the investors had invited me to a meeting <u>with the express intention of enlisting me in an effort to help salvage their interest in the situation</u>. I have a reputation of being able to quickly assess and turn around tough situations. I was not there because I am a marginally decent accountant or an expert on process mapping. They were concerned that they were going to lose the investment and wanted my help.

I do not remember much of the rest of the meeting. The light that went on between my ears was blinding to everything other than the realization that I had discovered a possible way of thinking about investing that might explain much of the failure I was regularly seeing.

Victim Mentality

I came to realize that the investors I was talking to - partners in a major venture capital firm - saw themselves as radically subservient to the management of the portfolio company. No, it was worse than that - they saw themselves as hostages - as victims without recourse. My mind raced from one description to another - trying to get the thought under some sort of control. I am completely sure that my hosts took my demeanor as evidencing a lack of interest in further discussions. Although that was true, it was not the primary driver of my behavior.

In the past, I had written about companies as growing children - offspring of the founders. The company would develop much as a child does - initially very dependent on the wisdom and support of the parent but eventually seeking its own way. This is a variation of the idea of 'complex self-organizing systems' put forth by the complexity theorists. Surely, there was something of this in the relationship between an investor and a portfolio company. However, further reflection lead me to discard this approach. Even the most engaged angel investors seemed to be little more than the equivalent of a 'rich uncle' who provides money out of a sense of something approximating familial obligation. There had to be a more productive way of looking at the process.

Shortly after my quasi-epiphany, I was having drinks with another investor - this time an angel who had invested in many companies. I described my earlier conversation and gathered another piece of the puzzle. *"When I invest, I invest in people and their abilities. The decision to provide funding is often the last major one that I make."*

I will admit that, as this person spoke, a vision of a casino and a craps table came to mind. Once the dice are tossed, the gambler is merely an onlooker just like everybody else around the table. The difference is that he - and some of the other onlookers - has an economic stake in the outcome. With the dice in hand, the investor is master of his own fate. Once the dice are thrown, he is just another paying passenger on the bus. Maybe one of the problems with investing was that investors see it as gambling - taking a chance on an idea and a team.

The combined vision was highly seductive - 'a rich uncle tossing dice'. However, it glossed over the relationship between the investor and the founders. Craps is an arrangement between the gambler and the casino - one that insures that the casino always wins in the end. Surely, the casino is grateful for the gamblers presence and their willingness to engage in what can only be a losing effort in the end. Sure, there are the occasional winners that make each gambler green with envy and fill them with the hope that they will be the next 'lucky one'.

However, in this case the game seemed rigged differently. The investor was maneuvered into the role of the casino and the founders were successfully rigging the game to mitigate their downside while preserving their upside. Can you imagine a casino accepting this arrangement? The gamblers are allowed to set the rules and the house only wins when the gamblers hit it big. In the meantime, the house insures them against losses. Casinos are not normally underwriters of such insurance.

What was missing was a plausible explanation of the dynamics of the relationship between the investor and founders. As I thought about these two interpretations, something stood out about them. In both cases - the gambler and the rich uncle - they were victims - victims who, by their own choice, had entered into an arrangement that was considerably less advantageous than zero-sum.

Probing the Power Imbalance

As I thought about the dynamics that seemed to define the investing experience, I came to suspect that the root causes were somehow embedded in the ritualized relationship between investors and the founders. There was something counter-logical about the patterns. It took me a while to work out a viable hypothesis. A key idea came from my five-year sabbatical from business and urban life. I had left New York City after some eighteen years and decided to buy a farm in Maryland. There I became a shepherd. The hundred acres supported a flock of two hundred sheep and kept four border collies and me working round the clock. One of my fondest memories from that time was training the dogs to work stock.

A productive dog is a combination of breeding, experience and a grasp of the dynamics among the dog, shepherd and flock - a dynamic that generally has a purpose attached. We might be shedding part of the flock for breeding, or putting them through the pens for worming - or maybe moving the entire flock to another pasture - so the fourth component was a solid grasp of the overall objective.

During those years, I ran training classes for people who had collies and wanted to improve their skills on stock. My problem students all had a variation of the same problem - they could not seem to reach a productive understanding with their dogs. I used to joke that the men had the problem because they insisted on treating their dogs as they treated their wives while the women insisted on treating their dogs as they treated their children. The point is that a productive relationship between a shepherd and dog recognizes the important contributions of each - and the contribution of the shepherd is not limited to providing the food at the end of the day.

With all this rolling through my mind, I headed out to the local park. It was a sunny, early spring day and the weather was fine. I took along my notepad and a good cigar. (I have found that there is at least one good idea in the first half-inch of any good one.) As I sat on the bench contemplating, two stories from my past came to visit.

Two Stories That Relate - Kind Of

Jim's Friend

One of my dearest friends was a lawyer who built the largest law firm in Florida. Jim had a tendency to attract interesting people and my visits to Jacksonville were often enlivened by that tendency. Over the years, I had been introduced to one particular friend. This person was towards the end of a very successful business life. I remember one morning meeting over breakfast. He was reflecting on parts of his life and regaling us with stories of business deals and other adventures in the Caribbean. For some reason the discussion turned to consultants and, seeing a chance to pour a bit of kerosene on the bonfire, I asked, "*what do you think of consultants?*" He leaned back and with an impish gleam in his eyes said, "*Ah consultants - yes. At the start, I have the money and they have the experience. After it is all over, I have the experience and they have the money.*"

Bears of the Pedernales

As it happened, a Texas businessman was in the habit of taking a couple of friends out for a weekend of bear hunting. He would drive them out Friday evening, set up a camp, enjoy time around the campfire, turn in and then wake early for a day of hunting. On this particular weekend, he took along his banker and a consultant. They arrived at the campsite and set up the tent. After a good dinner and fireside camaraderie, they turned in.

At first light, the Texan was awakened by shouting that seemed to be coming from outside the tent. He pried open one eye and looked over at the banker - still asleep. Then he glanced over at the consultant's cot and found it empty. As the fog of sleep began to recede, the shouting became more distinct. He realized that it was the consultant and he was shouting, "*Open the tent - open the tent*".

The businessman rolled out of his cot and threw back the tent flap. There, about twenty feet away, was the consultant coming at him as fast as his legs could manage. About twenty feet behind the consultant was a very large and clearly irritated bear. As the consultant ran into the tent and out the far end, he yelled, "*You take care of this one and I'll go get another one!*"

~~~~~~~~~~~~~~~~~~~~

Neither of the protagonists in the stories was likely to cease employing consultants. However, both had a good appreciation of how wasteful and dangerous they can be if left to their own devices. There was something in those two anecdotes that seemed to relate to my inquiry.

It seems to me that the more proactive you are in setting expectation and defining metrics, the more productive a consultant might be. Executives who take a 'hands off' approach are most likely to have less productive experiences with consultants. The 'it's all Geek to me' approach can be very expensive. Executives who are more proactive in forming and directing the engagement are more likely to feel that the investment in the consultant was worthwhile. Of course, at the extreme, those executives may end up doing the consultant's work or micro managing the process to irrelevance. It is, after all, a question of balance.

Another piece of the puzzle showed up. The correct power balance between an executive and consultant is that the executive defines expectations and expected results. The consultant delivers on those results or is not paid. In situations where the power balance is reversed - the consultant is running the engagement and the executive is reduced to a source of currency - the results tend to be far less likely to be acceptable.

This line of thought led me to consider the power balance between investors and founders. Over the next couple of weeks, I talked to or had meetings with a number of investors - both angel investors and venture capitalists. During those meetings, a pattern began to emerge - a pattern of a power

balance that directly contradicted the
appropriate dynamics of the situation.

Radical Imbalance

Over the last decade, I have had a front row seat at a number of what I now call 'radical power imbalance morality plays'. The cast of characters is nearly always the same. There is the 'hero' - the lead founder who is successfully feeding his team off the body of the investor. Then there is the team - the gathered leaches who feed at the trough and deliver little of value short of the gas they pass as a result of their gluttony. Finally, there is the host to these parasites - the complicitous investor - the one who makes all this waste possible. Like the living prey of a spider - caught firmly in a web of circumstance and having its life gradually - then not so gradually - sucked away.

Not a pretty sight is it. However, that is what it has amounted to in these cases. The curse is the lost opportunity - the 'I could have been a contender' sense of tragedy that overhangs almost all of these kamikaze raids on vacant lots. Without the imposition of discipline and strong performance metrics, inexperienced founders take the easy way out of a situation that threatens to be profoundly challenging. Given two options - the first to undertake the hard and risky business of building a company and the second the much easier road of exchanging excuses for income - most opt for the current income.

Under conditions of radical imbalance, the investor is merely a handmaiden to the princess - a provider of resources to an indolent and pretentious spoiled child. However - and here's the rub - the child is not of its own creation. The investor creates the brat - coddles it like an overindulgent parent - tells it that it is indeed special among all children - overlooks its faults and subsidizes its stupidities.

You Get What You Tolerate

The dilemma an angel investor is
sometimes profound but far more often
quite pedestrian. They certainly do not want
to run the company - why then would you
have founders? It is inherently dangerous to
take the gambler's pose and trust to fate
and chance. As with most things, the
answer is somewhere in the middle.
However, one thing has become clear to
me. It is the actions and attitudes of the
investor that creates. The founders are
merely opportunists. Although it may be
their last major contribution to the process,
investors set the ship firmly on a course
that is rife with icebergs - cluttered with
rampant with rapids - and destined mostly
for failure. Be careful what you wish for -
but watch carefully what you tolerate - nay,
insist on.

Hard Choices or Hard Times

In Angel's Sins, I outlined some of the mistakes that early stage investors make. When I published an abbreviated version of the chapter, I received quite a few responses from investors - some that contain tales of woe and loss while others invited me to 'get involved' in an effort to salvage what can be saved of a lost situation. The common theme in these comments was something like "*you are talking about me and my experiences aren't you*". Quite a few of my angel investor friends had to be reassured that the 'sins' were much more widely committed than they had realized. I do not much like these latter invitations - too hard on the digestion with little to show when it comes to results. Treating sick puppies may be necessary but this book is about a preventive approach.

The message that I deliver when I speak to groups of early-stage investors is that they have to look to their own tendencies. Physicians heal thyself! Their options are hard choices or hard times. If they do not take a firm, focused and demanding approach to setting and enforcing the terms surrounding their investments, they turn the whole process into a rolling of the dice - and that is more like gambling than investing.

Most angel investors seem to approach the

process with a kind of 'grandfatherly'
attitude - or, perhaps, like a 'rich uncle' who
is supporting the 'younger generation' with
their favors and support. The damage this
'gentle' and 'disconnected' approach can do
is hard to overstate. Life understandings
are 'softened' and rendered formless.
Understandings that might support a career
of success and accomplishment are turned
away - and the result is failure where
success should have been.

If you are getting the sense that this chapter
is more about the negative impact on the
recipients of angel investment, you are
right. I have seen this benign neglect and
'grandfatherly' soft-soap ruin both
businesses and careers.

~~~~~~~~~~~~~~~~~~~~~~~~~~~~~~~~~~~

Lies by Yevgeny Yevtushenko

Lying to the young is wrong.
Proving to them that lies are true is wrong.
Telling them that God's in his heaven and
all's well with the world is wrong.
They know what you mean. They are
people too.
Tell them the difficulties can't be counted,
and let them see not only what will be but
see with clarity these present times.
Say obstacles exist they must encounter,
sorrow comes, hardship happens.
The hell with it. Who never knew the price
of happiness will not be happy.

Forgive no error you recognize, it will repeat itself, a hundredfold and afterward our pupils will not forgive in us what we forgave.

~~~~~~~~~~~~~~~~~~~~~~~~~~~~~~~~~

Yevtushenko is saying something important - something angel investors should have tattooed on the inside of their eyelids. Business is not just difficult to get right - only one in ten start-ups make it to their fifth anniversary - most CEOs may understand the business of their business - it is that these CEOs do not adequately understand the business of business. The very people who could and should be teaching them the need for discipline, veracity, focus, and exacting attention to detail - are smiling benevolently like some Cheshire Cat.

I am not one out to change the world, as we know it. I have long ago come to the realization that people are going to change slowly and only under focused and concerted pressure. My work with early-stage investors focuses on getting them to accept the need for effective, direct and often stiff adult supervision. In my book _Amazing Pace: Turbo-Charged Business Development_, I describe how this adult supervision can be arranged for the business development process. The pattern suggested in that book applies here as well.

In my writings about governance and oversight, I have focused on demonstrating how important a professionally organized board of directors can be in determining the future prospects of a company. The first function of such a board is to provide the necessary 'adult supervision' - set and enforce the standards for performance.

When I write about my advisory work with CEOs, I argue that the kind of direct and firm guidance that an experienced serial entrepreneur can bring to the table can provide a template - and example - for the aspiring entrepreneur. It also supplies the demand for accountability, veracity and a commitment to results that goes well beyond the verbal.

Failure is a much sadder tail if it is the result of indifference, missed opportunities and regrets for what might have been. Investors advance their own interests by making sure that there is a firmness - even forcefulness - in the mentoring of the CEOs and management teams they have invested in.

~~~~~~~~~~
Hard Choices that Lead to Better Times
~~~~~~~~~~

Yevtushenko has a point that all angel investors should take to heart. The best way to improve the chances of success is by forcing the CEO and senior team to come to terms with how hard it is to succeed - to make sure that they have an immediate and visceral experience of what is necessary to make a go of the business. Investors should take the lead in highlighting the hard choices. They should then insist - persistently - that these hard choices be met and overcome through well thought-out and implemented solutions. No other contribution is as important as this one - hold managements' feet to the fire until they learn how to control and channel that fire. In my role as advisor to investors, I regularly organize and facilitate 'red-team' sessions that do exactly that. Here are some of the issues that regularly are a part of those sessions:

I do not believe your projections. Convince me that they are an accurate reflection of the results you are going to generate.
I do not accept that your sales strategy will be effective. What evidence do you have that it will succeed? Your record of accomplishment (or lack of record of accomplishment) in sales does not give me comfort. The entire future of the company rests on the ability to generate sales - build an expanding customer base.

I think you have underestimated the difficulties in the competitive marketplace. You do not seem to have a strong familiarity with your competition? (I generally do quite a bit of research in this area and come to the sessions with a more thoroughgoing knowledge of the competition than the CEO and senior team have)

I do not think that you really understand the decision process and points of pain of your potential customers. How are you going to convinced them - in an environment of scarce resources and funding - that they need to forego other options and subscribe to your value proposition?

I do not think that your team is 'A' players. It may be technologically strong enough but where is the revenue going to come from? Is it a team that can turn the value proposition into revenue?

I do not think that you have a sufficient knowledge of potential disruptive technologies that will render your value proposition obsolete. How are you going to keep up with the crest of the wave?

The investors are in this for a return on their investment. How are your efforts going to assure that? My suspicion is that you are more focused on building the business than meeting their needs.

The purpose of these sessions is to focus the minds of the management team and the investors on a commonly held vision of the company. They also identify key areas where the staffing, technology, strategic and tactical plans and resourcing of the company are inadequate to the challenges. By addressing and mastering the hard choices early on, a culture develops from the beginning that faces challenges directly. There is then a lesser tendency to 'dance away' from them. The 'head-in-the-sand' ostrich tendencies are flushed out of the company.

I cannot emphasize too strongly, how important it is to take this approach from the very beginning. Habits are formed through living - habits that lead to a successful business - happy experience for investors - are forged in the heat of confronting hard choices and overcoming them.

The 'Elevator Speech' Antidote

Listening to the delivery of an elevator speech is the single most distracting event in an investor's journey. It is to that point in time - the equivalent of 'love at first sight' - that most of the subsequent failures can be traced. An elevator speech is an exercise in advertising. It is an attempt to draw a potential investor in and get them interested in providing funding for a venture. In the starkest terms, it is a money trap.

Because of their brevity, elevator speeches are selective in their focus. They dance away from - or avoid all together - issues that undermine the apparent viability of the value proposition on offer. The necessarily simplified approach begins with an assumption that the presenter and team is able to execute - monetize the value proposition - and that their ideas are their own. In stark terms, an elevator speech is a swindle - a created illusion that - necessarily - avoids or minimizes potential lethal challenges and highlights a series of yet to be tested and usually overly optimistic assumptions.

If you are getting the impression that I have a strong aversion to the entire idea of elevator speeches, you are correct. Investors have lost more money because they failed to critically evaluate and aggressively test key underlying assumptions than for any other reason.

This single misstep is by far the biggest 'company killer' in the process. In a recent article - Assumption is the Mother of All … - Lessons for Young Wannabees - I argued that untested assumptions are the primary reason that most start-ups fail. Here I would add that untested assumptions are the primary reason that most investments in start-ups go south.

Here is a series of questions that I recommend any angel investor push hard on before then even considering providing money for a start-up:

Why should I think that you are capable of building and running a business? Prove to me that you understand the business of business - not just the business of your intended business. Repeatedly I have encountered companies whose CEO was very good at promoting themselves and the idea behind the company - they were masters at the kind of shallow-water thinking that goes into creating a good elevator speech - but a complete failure at assembling, managing and leading a professional and effective team. Investors have to ask the hard questions early on and challenge the assumption that the elevator speaker can build and run a successful company. The hard truth is that most of them cannot.

Who is on your team that would impress me and what kind of a deal did you have to make to get them onboard? I will want to talk to them - to see if they are floaters or workers. What have they accomplished since joining the team? I am surprised at the percentage of sociopaths that find their way into becoming CEOs. Primarily they are of two kinds. The first is not comfortable with the idea that 'there are other people on the planet'. They are more comfortable with 'ideas' and 'concepts'. As a result, they constantly are moving the flatware around on the table - but cannot seem to assemble a team dedicated to their ideas. The second are the 'uncritical assemblers'. These people are good at piling up names but, when you start poking around the team, you find that the dedication to - and often understanding of - the value proposition behind the company is somewhat gossamer. These entrepreneurs are not able to build effective and dedicated teams. They are talk show hosts and always very bad investments.

Do not tell me about your passion - tell me about your accomplishments. I am not looking for the glib or theatrical. What have you already done to turn your ideas into a going business? If the answer is nothing of substance, come back then you have. Passion is one of those buzz words that simply will not go away. In my experience, it is a poor substitute for other, more important, ingredients. I prefer an entrepreneur who is focused, persistent, knowledgeable, determined and who makes the best use the resources at their disposal. The illusion of passion can be manufactured - most educated people are adept at it - but these other things cannot.

Do not tell me about markets. Who are your customers? Amateurs have markets - pros have customers. Who believes in your ideas enough to pay for them? This one really drives me nuts. Somebody sends me a business plan and I get to the section that is supposed to be focused on the possibility of revenues and encounter something like the following. "The total market is XXXXX billions of dollars annually and if we get even one tenth of one percent of that … (blah, blah, blah)". This is a simple bait and switch - an investor is baited with a huge number - then shifted to accepting the ability - and, most often as it turns out, the inability - of the team to implement in a way that captures any part of that huge number at all.

Do not tell me about your revenue model - tell me about your revenue. I do not trust Excel spreadsheets - projections are usually self-serving crap. Tell me about your revenues to date. CEOs that are not dedicated to generating revenues from the very beginning need to be avoided. I recently reviewed a 'business plan' that admitted that the company would be cash flow negative through at least two follow-on capital raises. In other words, if the company were not able to raise the additional capital, the investors would lose their investment. The message behind the business plan was, "we are too busy doing product development to dirty our hands chasing revenues." These are not companies - they are science projects. If you want to supply grant money, go ahead. If you expect a return on your investment, dream on.

Do not go on about differentiators or competitive advantage; tell me about a customer that you took from another company. It is not ideas that I am interested in - its implementation. Show me that you have implemented your ideas - stolen customers - generated revenues. This point relates to the one above. No validation of the value proposition is relevant unless it comes from a customer who has paid real money for what the company has on offer. The real test of the validity of the value proposition is the market - not the investors or the founders.

Slow down - I am not interested in being the focus of a heated rush. If you think your business can be described in a few sentences, you are far more simple-minded than the world as I know it. I often suspect that 'entrepreneur wannabees' who are good at elevator speeches suffer from ADD. Their attention span is so short that the brevity of an elevator speech is all they can manage. Their vision of business, their business and the investor's world is so abbreviated that anything beyond instant gratification and casual agreements escapes them. Getting a CEO beyond the elevator speech and into deeper waters is one of the best ways to test their ability to build and manage a company.

Recent trends and the economic downturn have made this an unfavorable time to seek financing. You do realize that, if we do reach an agreement, the valuation of your so-called company will be very low and I will end up owning most of it until you can produce results that allow you to buy it back. I occasionally receive packages on pre-revenue companies with proposed valuations in the millions. My response is always the same - set the valuation at the investment amount and allow the management team to buy in through sweat equity and results. Initially the investors will own most of the company but, with success, the management team can increase their share of ownership. Most investors are very happy to allow the team to achieve a majority position - if they earn it.

These are just a sample of the questions that I recommend investors ask when reviewing a potential investment. Pressing them will improve your returns. If you cannot bring yourself to press them, bring in somebody who can. Whatever they cost, you will be a small matter compared to losing your entire investment.

After the Elevator Ride

My first recommendation after hearing a really good elevator speech is 'take a break' - four or five days at a minimum. Then sit down and outline the key components of the pitch. Use them as initial testing points. Good questions to ask are:

Who is this person and why should I believe anything they say? Do not stop with the visceral reaction. Burrow down into their reputation. Check around - use your network to gather information about others' experiences. Ask for and check references carefully.

What do I know about the business? Two hours of focused Googling will give you an initial survey of the space. Try to bracket the value proposition. Do not stop with the competitors. Burrow into the suppliers, look closely at the intended customer base and spend time looking for disruptive technologies.

What can you find out about the other members of the team? Again, check reputations and references. If you find out that most of the players are neophytes, you need to be particularly careful. I am particularly wary of gatherings of 'consultants'. For the most part, consultants are not team players.

What other propositions are floating around in this space? It is very rare that one person will come up with a totally novel idea. Try to separate your response to the value proposition from that of the founders. Many a good investments is lost when a good idea in the hands of an inept team produces a losing business. If, after doing some diligence, you find the value proposition particularly compelling, you may want to search for a better founder and team to implement it.

Gather your own team of experts. Use your network to recruit a team of 'reviewers'. Many times, they will see what you have missed.

The key to the process is to 'forget' the elevator speech as soon as possible. An organized and focused diligence process will help you do just that. Roll up your sleeves and delve into the details of the value proposition. Test every assumption. Start with the attitude 'this can't be right' and you will make for progress that is much more reliable. Delve into the backgrounds of all the people on the team. Pay particular attention to the capabilities and skill set of the founders. Look for 'blind spots' that might undercut their ability to build and manage the kind of team necessary to make a go of it. Again, accept nothing on its face. Burrow down to solid ground - question everything.

If you follow this process, you will gain two kinds of very valuable information. First, you will be better able to assess the team and value proposition. Second - and just as important - you will learn something important about the founders. The ones who just do not seem to have patience for that kind of detailed diligence or do not have clear and well-based answers to your questions are probably not going to be capable of building and running a business.

Governance

Most angel investors, when funding a start-up, ignore the structure and operation of the board of directors. Most early-stage companies that I work with have only a casually structured board that seems to exist to satisfy legal requirements. Accumulated experience has shown me that this is a very risky approach. A board has defined obligations that are important to the future of any company. Boards unable to fulfill these obligations severely limit possibilities. Here are some of the guidelines that I offer when working with these start-ups:

Composition: A well-functioning board is independent of the management team. I have an aversion to CEOs who also hold the title of Chairman of the Board. A board, which is simply a rubber stamp or doormat, creates an imbalance within the organization's culture - key functions are untended or receive short shrift. A functioning board should have a majority of independent members. In my view, the term independent excludes both members of the senior team <u>and</u> investors.

Balance: All the rhetoric aside, the tendencies of management are inherently tactical and self-serving. The CEO is - or should be - focused on implementing the strategic and tactical plans. All implementation is inherently tactical. The team's compensation - if it is correctly structured - should focus heavily on meeting those metrics and delivering on the plans. Even the most experienced CEOs work this way. That implies an unbalanced emphasis on the tactical. An independent board acts as a counterbalance to this tendency.

Professional Members: Board members need to have the accumulated experience and refined judgment that will allow them to help formulate and monitor an effective strategic plan. Their vision needs to be long-term. They fulfill their fiduciary responsibility to the shareholders by balancing short-term tactical issues with longer-term ones. One of the changes that I have seen in recent years is a tendency among angel investors to seek out professional board members to take the seats that their investment entitles them to. Angel investors can draw on two pools of talent. The first is successful serial entrepreneurs and the second is professionally trained directors. Both bring important knowledge and experience to the board - both add significantly to the corporate culture.

The Business of Business: As I have written elsewhere, most start-ups fail (one in ten makes it to their fifth anniversary) because the team fails at the business of business. Most start-up teams have a good grasp of the business of their business. A well-functioning board will help make sure that the 'non-technology' aspects of the start-up are not the ones that bring it down. One of the most important of these is oversight - both strategic and tactical. Professional board members have the experience to tell when a management team is blowing smoke or missing the point. They also have the 'stiffness' to confront the CEO and force the necessary changes.

Standards and Metrics: One of the biggest dangers in a start-up is constantly moving goalposts. The double diversions of constantly evolving Power Point slide stacks and constantly reworked Excel spreadsheets can eliminate the possibility of holding the management team to any metrics at all. A functioning board will insist that performance meet projections and aggressively oppose the proposition that projections should be adjusted to match performance. The latter is one of the most serious diseases that can infect any start-up. A management team that constantly lowers expectations to match failure is an amateurish gaggle.

Holding to Account: In simple terms, if you cannot say what you are going to do and then do it, what is your word really worth? If you say you are a CEO, make statements about what your team is going to accomplish which induce investors to risk wealth based on those statements and them fail to deliver on those statements, you are not a CEO - you are a highwayman. A well-functioning board will detect these bandits and take steps to replace them with people that are more professional and productive.

There is a tendency to overlook the impact of governance on the fortunes of start-up companies. My view is that this is a mistake. A well-structured and focused board significantly improves the prospects of any start-up. The cost of such a board is incidental when compared to the risks that it helps control and overcome. 'Adult supervision' alone is worth the investment. However, the other benefits - such as a wider range of contacts, introductions to important decision-makers, support in implementing effective control systems, professional evaluation of performance and more, make a well-functioning board one of the most valuable assets any start-up can have.

Board Assessment

A professionally functioning board plays a central role in the management of any company. Its principal obligation is to manage the business in the best interest of the shareholders. The primary and fiduciary obligation of board members is first to protect and extend shareholder value. In the scheme of things, the board works for the shareholders and management works for, and at the pleasure of, the board.

In broader terms, the board acts on behalf of the shareholders. It is responsible for establishing operating policies, making sure that the right CEO has operational responsibility and for overseeing the management of the company - insuring that it operates within the limits of all existing law and in the best interest of its stockholders.

Recent corporate scandals have shown what can happen when boards neglect this obligation. Legislation has attempted to re-balance the power dynamics in public companies. These efforts have had an impact on corporate governance and the role and responsibility of boards. An increased understanding of the critical role played by these boards has begun to spread beyond public companies. In the years that followed the passage of Sarbanes-Oxley, investors in early-stage companies have begun to focus on the need to have a fully functioning and professionally organized board of directors. Investors in these companies have an increasing appreciation for the necessity of standing up such a board early in a company's history.

Occasionally I assess the operations of boards of directors. The request typically comes from a shareholder - most often an investor who sees a company generating poorer results than either expected or desired. Over the years, I have developed a checklist that guides these assessments. I conduct assessments methodically - working through a list - systematically developing answers to a series of questions.

Is the board independent? By this I do not mean a board that has a majority of 'outside directors' - I mean a board that has no directors who are part of the management team. Management does have a role in Board functioning. It presents for approval. There is an inherent conflict of roles when a sitting director passes judgment on management proposals if that director is also a member of the management team. The term 'rubber stamp' comes to mind. The board represents the interests of the shareholders in such matters and, in that role, needs to be free of the many pressures which management deals with - such as maximizing compensation and equity accumulation.

Is the Chairman also the CEO? I have written elsewhere about the corrosive effects of this combination of roles. The role of the Chairman inherently conflicts with that of the CEO. The Chairman must assure that the board meets its fiduciary obligations to the shareholders. The board sits in judgment of management. It assures that the company has the right management team and, particularly, the right CEO. It doesn't seem adventurous to assert that such a review process being led by the CEO will tend towards the affirmative.

Does the Board have a Succession Plan? Is there a succession plan in place? Such a plan does not necessarily mean that the board is intending to replace the CEO in the near future. Good governance recognizes that the process of 'bringing along' candidates takes time. The existence of a plan is an indication that the board is focusing on the need to assure continuity of quality leadership. Most plans provide for a response to the 'dropped out of the sky' eventuality. "What would happen to the company is the CEO died tomorrow?" It also should deal with the ability of the CEO to reinvent themselves as the company grows - as its needs become both more complex and more focused - and the role that the CEO needs to play comes to focus more on the business of business and less on the business of the business. Many topnotch start-up CEOs simply cannot make this journey - and their companies suffer because of it.

About a third of the time a start-up company has the right CEO. It is that rare that the stars align to bring a good ideas and the right person to implement them together. For the rest, about half will have an entrepreneur who may be capable of taking the company from launch to its first major need to restructure - generally to about one to five million in run-rate. After that, the CEO will have to be replaced or the company will stagnate and turn into a life-style company with limited potential. For the balance, the entrepreneur is not up to the task of successfully launching the company. Sometimes this is because they have the wrong skill-sets. With others, it is the wrong disposition.

Although this analysis may seem harsh, it is important to remember that one in ten start-up companies make it to their fifth anniversary. Ninety percent go out of business before that. Of that ten percent, less than half achieve a twenty million dollar run rate. Most of these failures come because management is unable to implement - to adequately monetize the value proposition. The board's primary responsibility is to protect and extend shareholder value and their first obligation is to make sure that the right CEO is running the shop. Succession planning is the instrument for meeting that obligation.

Does the Board Provide Effective Compensation Planning and Oversight? I recently encountered a company where the CEO arbitrarily gave himself and other team members raises. What was striking about the situation? Well, the raises were granted on the sole authority of the CEO - without board approval - and the management team had just finished a quarter where results were twenty-five percent of projections.

A good compensation scheme ties levels to performance and incentivizes management when it performs above expectations. That said, all compensation schemes have a heavily tactical emphasis. Even the best focus primarily on near-term results. This is particularly true in start-up situations where the long term limited by the resources available.

Because cash is such a dear commodity in most start-ups, compensation schemes become particularly important. Labor is often the largest expense category and needs to be aggressively controlled. I have encountered start-up companies with bloated teams being paid salaries that might be appropriate if the company was doing twenty million in annual sales. These pre-revenue companies had a culture based on the idea of entitlement. I remember discussing one such company with an old friend and long-time mentor. After I had finished laying out the details, Jim shook his head and muttered, "Never have so many been paid so much to deliver so little!" I am thinking of having it tattooed on the inside of my eyelids.

Does the Board Provide Effective Audit Oversight? Recently I had to 'make up' a 1099 for my tax return. Management had decided not to issue them. I suppose they thought they were doing me a favor. I did not see it that way.

Larcenous tendencies can corrupt a corporate culture. Like dry rot, it can start as an innocuous way and quickly spread. Failure to comply with clear obligations can indicate a tendency to cut corners and make convenient compromises. The discipline of accounting is one of the first that any management team encounters and the Audit Committee of the Board is responsible for seeing that they submit to that discipline.

An audit committee has a responsibility that extends beyond simply reviewing and approving the company's financials. It needs to assure the board and shareholders that appropriate controls and oversight are in place - controls on and oversight focuses on management. I occasionally encounter companies where the CEO has single signature authority over the operating account - and, in rare occasions, over the credit lines. This is not just a recipe for disaster - it constitutes a gross dereliction of duty - negligence on the part of the board.

So Much from So Few: If you are presently involved in a start-up, you are probably thinking, "We barely have a functioning board of directors, how can we few cover all these bases?" I understand that it may be difficult - but you need to accept that it must be done. Investments are lost and companies fail mostly because management and the board underperform when it comes to the business of business - the business of building and running a business. When prudence and best practices are abandoned, a start-up becomes less about entrepreneurial activity and more akin to a game of chance - with heavy odds in favor of disaster.

Is the Board the final judge on the strategic plans advanced by management? One of the most important roles of the board is to evaluate - and adjust where necessary - the strategic plans proposed by management. If it is functioning correctly, the board provides the final, critical review of these plans. As part of their fiduciary responsibility to protect and extend shareholder value, the board must review the plan with the shareholders' interests in mind. This is a critical contribution to good governance and the future of the company for three reasons.

First, it counterbalances the tendency of management to think tactically and in their self-interest. As most compensation schemes are short-term focused, management will tend prefer plans that maximize their total compensation by adopting tactical approaches recast as 'strategic' ones. There is nothing inherently wrong with this approach. Acting on self-interest is a fundamental underpinning of capitalism. However, there must be an effective check on this tendency.

Second, the board represents a much longer-term view than management. As a friend used to put it, shareholders are the owners, management are renters. The strategic challenges that any company faces generally divide into two broad categories. The first is the need to stay relevant to their customers - continually refine the value proposition. For the most part, management tends to be better at this process than the second one - managing the company through its various stages of growth and reinvention. The long view of the board will force a balanced planning and resourcing process, which will improve the chances that the company will not only survive but also thrive long after the current management team, has retired.

Third, the board acts as a reviewer-of-last-resort. It should regularly assess the effectiveness of management - its attempts to monetize the value proposition - manage the company in the shareholders' interest - implement the strategic plan - etc. Remember, the board serves at the pleasure of the shareholders - management serves at the pleasure of the board. The board is the executive body - the formally constituted agent of the shareholders. It is they, not management who are ultimately responsible to the shareholders. Every strategic initiative, plan, decision, collaboration, acquisition or financing proposed by management should be reviewed and approved by the board. The board should enforce every decision made by vote of the shareholders.

Is the Board in a cooperative rather than collaborative relationship with management? A friend uses the term 'creative tension' to describe a cooperative relationship. A cooperative relationship is professional and non-conspiratorial. Roles are distinct and the tension exists because the differing roles require differing agendas, priorities and actions.

One of the major reasons that I prefer a completely independent board is the impossibility of serving the two masters - the interest of management in maximizing their compensation and the interest of the shareholders in protecting and extending shareholder value. The principal driver of conflict here is between management's interest in receiving 'appropriate' compensation for their contributions and the board's need to assure that compensation is neither excessive nor inappropriately focused. To put it in starker terms, from the board's perspective, every dollar that is paid to management is a reduction of shareholder value that needs to be more than matched by an increase in shareholder value as a result of management's contributions - management has to be a 'good buy'. From management's perspective, every dollar that comes to them helps to pay the mortgage, buy the new car and send the kids to the 'right schools'.

These dynamics clash in the relationship between management and the board. A well-functioning board balances two perspectives - the relatively short-term and self-interested interests of management and the relatively longer-term and self-interested interests of shareholders. The board must manage the tension that these two competing views create. In the end, board members must give preference to the interests of the shareholders. They are, after all, representatives of the shareholders and employers of management.

Does the Board meet its fiduciary obligations to the shareholders? The board works for the shareholders - management works at the direction of the board. That is the simple and accurate description of the law governing corporate governance. I am constantly amazed at how far from reality situations often become.

The extreme variation is 'the board is a vassal of management - a rubber stamp - and the shareholders are passive and, for the most part, unrepresented in the process of governance'. Over the years I wondered how this could so frequently come to be - what set of circumstances could conspire to turn the process of governance so completely around. Accumulated evidence and experience has driven me to the unavoidable conclusion that it is the attitude of shareholders - investors - that has allowed this perversion to become so common. For the most part, they have been getting what they deserved.

This might sound a bit harsh, I know. However, I would counsel a bit of reflection before questioning its inaccuracy. There are four primary drivers of this attitude and each of them places investors in a servile relationship with the management of the companies they invested in.

The first is a lemming mentality. Investors tend to group together and share 'war stories'. They tend to set patterns of behavior that reinforces the power of the entrepreneurs over themselves.

The second is their susceptibility to the charm of an entrepreneur's elevator pitch.

Personally, I have little use for such 'simple-minded' presentations. Many angel investors seem to be positively addicted to them. Business is never 'simple-minded' and value propositions that can be reduced to 'elevator speeches' or a slide stack should be avoided. The devil really is in the details - and most investments are lost because of a failure to ask the hard, complex questions and tie funding to adequate answers and incentivized implementation.

The third tendency that leads to this inversion of governance is the 'grandfatherly' approach that most angel investors take to their investments. This one drives me completely nuts. Maybe they are just too old or tired - maybe they have lost the ability to focus - perhaps Alzheimer's is setting in. They give a kid a loaded gun, pat them on the head and say 'now be a nice kid and go out and play'. Governance is just as important during the start-up phase as it is in the mature phase of corporate growth. The single difference is that many more outcomes that are possible are lethal to investor interests earlier on.

The fourth tendency comes at the confluence of greed and indolence. Investors are in such a hurry to 'capture' the next and greatest investment opportunity that they 'throw money' at entrepreneurs much like college coaches used to throw cars and hookers at high school stars.

Driven by a herd mentality, they often brag about 'snagging the deal' - often meaning that they were taken to the cleaners in a bigger way than their contemporaries would accept.

Imprudence on the part of investors assures an imprudent approach to governance and an ineffective board. This casual approach infects the culture of the management team. Without board oversight and guidance, start-up CEOs - most of who have limited experience in building a company - 'make it up as they go along'. In doing so, the virtually guarantee the failure of the company and the loss of investment.

Metrics

The curse of modern society is that we have attained a facility with language without learning how to use it effectively. We use words like 'metrics' as if we understand what they mean and how to implement their meaning. Repeatedly I encounter the same situation - principally created by investors. The poor management team is suffering from 'reporting overload'. In a recent engagement, the overload was driven by a byzantine structure of an Excel spreadsheet - or I say spreadsheets - that the investors had employed someone to concoct. It did not take much time to diagnose one of the principal reasons that the business was failing. Everyone - the CEO, management team, investors and the consultant that generated the obscenity - focused on comparing the results to a series of arcane and completely irrelevant metrics. The entire process produced but one result - continual and increasing levels of frustration.

I want to make it clear from the beginning that I am a strong advocate of metrics - clearly stated and enforced. The issue is not should there be metrics. The issue is 'what metrics should there be at various stages of a company's growth? I am advocating something along the lines of that Gilbert and Sullivan lyric from the Mikado:

My object all sublime
I shall achieve in time —
To let the punishment fit the crime —
The punishment fit the crime;

Measuring what matters at the time begins with an understanding of what matters at the time and then developing metrics that are appropriate to that time and condition of the company. In the very early stages of a start-up the focus should be on efficiency of the use of the scare resources - principally cash - and the progress made towards generating revenue.

Efficient Use of Resources: A start-up has a very limited number of critical resources and never enough of each. The first on the list is cash and/or credit. The amount available divided by the monthly cost of running the business determines the length of the 'runway' - that virtual track at the end of which is a brick wall that needs to be flown over if the company is to get off the ground. If the company runs out of cash before getting to the point that revenues will sustain it, the results will be one of two:

<u>It is all over - the effort did not pay out</u>. The investors will/should grab the intellectual property and perhaps will try to find another team to monetize the value proposition but it is over for the CEO and current team.

<u>The team goes on a hunt for additional</u>

financing. I once had a CEO ask me 'what is my company worth'. I could tell where he was going. I knew that he had run out of money and was negotiating with his investors for a follow-on round. My response was 'nothing - you are losing money and not making your projections'. As it turned out, the valuation used for the follow-on round was roughly twenty-five percent of the original valuation. The CEO had no choice by that time. He could have maintained a healthy percentage interest in the company by actually generating revenues sufficient to preclude the need for another round of investment. However, that had not happened.

Investors should take the lead in defining what 'effective use' means and codifying those meanings into clearly stated and enforceable metrics. I recommend that they first address the expense side of the equation. How much of the money is going out monthly to cover 'non-performance' compensation? Earlier I had referred to the tendency to compensate senior team members at non-contingent levels that are more appropriate for larger, better-established companies. The investors are giving that team a chance to build a company - and to benefit from having done so. The *quid pro quo* for that opportunity should be a subordination of the bulk of their compensation to their performance.

Recently an investor asked me for

guidelines in this area. "How much - what percentage - of a CEO's compensation should be dependent on hitting the numbers," he asked? My response was 75% to 80%. He just stared for a while then began again.

- Him: How are they supposed to live on that deal - pay the mortgage, buy food, pay for their cell phone?
- Me: By hitting the numbers and collecting 100% of their compensation.
- Him: But, my people never hit their numbers!
- Me: Then one of two things is the issue - wrong people or wrong expectations.

The arrangement that I outlined above has two principal benefits. The first is that it mitigates against the kind of 'pie-in-the-sky' projections that pass for 'representations-never-expected-to-be-met' that are so commonly produced by entrepreneurs trying to lure investors. A CEO who is willing to bet 80% of his compensation on meeting those projections is worth listening to. A CEO who is not is worth avoiding.

More importantly, set the culture in the company:

Developing and Refining the Metrics: When asked where I would start in defining metrics for a start-up, I generally respond 'expenses and revenues'. Recently, when I responded in that way, an investor replied, *"expenses we have a lot of - revenues we have none"*. I grimaced, took a breath and we went to work.

Revenues: The term 'pre-revenue' amuses me - what a charming euphemism - it is an obviously word-play on 'pre-dawn'. However, there is a key difference - the sun will most likely come up. When a CEO or investor uses the term, I offer my alternative - don't you mean 'no revenue'? Here I admit to being kind. My suggestion often ought to be 'no revenue and likely none ever'. You cannot image the number of science projects I come across that have little or no revenues and likely never will cover costs let alone show a profit.

I recently reviewed a company for an investor. The business plan was full of 'transformational' language. The company was going to 'change the world as we know it'. When I asked about revenues, I got an assurance that many of the companies who were conducting no-cost trials were likely to sign fat contracts 'any day now'. So how long had this company been offering and granting these no-cost pilot projects? Two years! The company was seeking its next round of funding. They were using the 'any day now' argument to pressure the investors into providing additional funds. Luckily, one of the investors was a pack rat - saved everything - including the Power

Point presentation used for the last funding round. There it was - 'any day now' - in a slide stack from over a year ago.

The problem that this company faced traced back to the way the investors cut their first deal with the CEO and senior team. With compensation based only on occupying the roles agreed to - there were no performance-contingent provisions - the CEO and senior team fulfilled the conditions of their employment - they went to the office, put in their time and (lacking any metrics that specified their obligations for fulfilling their obligations) settled down to product development that they felt more comfortable with. The experience was the proverbial 'self-fulfilling prophesy'.

The very first set of metrics should focus on tracking the results of revenue generation. After all, the investors are providing funding to create a business. Revenues separate business from science projects or eleemosynary institutions. The effective monetization of the value proposition is the principal reason for the company to exist at all.

Expenses: I am often amazed at how casually some entrepreneurs seem to take the opportunity that investors have given them - and how callously they treat the investment that they have made in the company. One of the most important metrics on the expense side of the equation is the percentage of expenses that go out the door whether the team is successful or not. I regularly encounter start-ups where this number is 100%. That means that, no matter what the results, the monthly burn rate remains the same. To say it another way, even in the face of failure the executives receive full compensation. Moreover, in the face of that failure, the investors see their capital washed away at a mind-numbingly constant pace. Where is the equity in that? In my book, all but the most essential compensation should be contingent on performance - period - paragraph.

Once the compensation metrics are in place, it is time to look at the other expenses. The big question focuses on whether or not expenditures are necessary for the advancement of the company and appropriate to its current and near-term condition. In a previous chapter, I described the tendency towards top-heavy management teams. If a company does not need a fulltime CFO or Vice President of Human Relations, the net effect of having either is an accelerated draining of cash reserves by overpayment for what might be appropriate two years down the road. The likelihood is, of course, that the company will run out of cash well before those skills are really needed.

One of the places I look first is the structure and operation of the sales effort. Two kinds of overspending are common. The first is what I call the roving gaggle. The office mostly empties out every time a sales call is made. In the early stages - when the CEO is operating as the lead salesperson - the tendency to take along the team can seem irresistible. In truth, it is draining and destructive. The culture that needs to dominate a good start-up is 'enough to win'. Generals might have the luxury of assembling overwhelming force before launching an assault but it is different for platoon commanders. In that situation, there are always more things that need doing than hands to do them. The same is true for a start-up.

The second type of overspending in this area is the 'unfocused and un-urgent' foray into the realm of potential clients. I have encountered CEOs who simply do not understand the value proposition from a potential client's point of view. I know that is the case - I regularly visit with potential clients at the beginning of my engagements. One CEO told me that he understood what the potential client needed better than they did. The condescending tone in his voice was the first giveaway that this was a reef to avoid. His potential clients were running successful businesses with million-dollar plus annual revenues. However, he knew better than they did what they needed - he who had yet to generate a cash-flow positive month!

A variation on this theme is what I call the 'sauntering sales effort'. This is the 'oh well, we'll get them next month' crowd. These people drive me completely nuts!! Every sales call adds to - or detracts from - the company's reputation. It is an early form of branding. If they wander into a decision-maker's office, give him the 'peter-powder-puff' version of your, get turned down and then fade out through the door, how long do you think it will be before he is on the phone to his contemporaries telling them what a gaggle of unfocused clowns you the CEO and team are?

Another place that I look is the budgeting for things like marketing and branding. An old mentor of mine was fond of saying "Son, you need something to brand before you can brand it. Branding what doesn't exist is just public masturbation. It may feel good to you but it's ugly to your audience." He was a salty old coot - and I learned a lot from him. Start-ups that spend scarce cash on marketing and branding - instead of sales and product development - are guilty of the same misspending sins that the companies I described in the paragraphs above.

Bang-for-the-buck is a good measure when it comes to setting metrics for expenses. '*If we spend this dollar, what will we reasonably expect to generate in returns?*' is a good question to always have at the forefront. Of course, the one to follow with is, '*Well, we spent that dollar in the hopes of generating that return. Is that what happened*?'

Use of funds: The normal way of looking at a start-up is as an airplane. The investment provides a 'runway'. The job of management is to get the plane airborne before they run out of runway. The weakness that I see in this approach is that the management team always seems to be working to find ways of extending the runway. If it is easier to raise additional funds than build a business … well you get the idea.

A better way to looking at the process may be as a multi-stage rocket. The investment is the booster stage - designed to get the thing off the ground and moving towards orbit. Boosters are normally solid fuel - and that seems a good analogy because in the early goings the only real solid thing in the equation is the funds provided. However, the boosters are designed to melt away early in the flight. It is the second stage that is important. That is normally a liquid fuel arrangement - and that seems appropriate because revenue is the liquid fuel of business. The key to a good rocket design - and to a well-managed start-up - is the smooth transition from the booster solid fuel to the second stage liquid stuff.

An important metric is the rate of transition from assisted take-off to self-sustaining flight. The marvelous thing about a business is that it can collect its own fuel in flight. By focusing management's attention of revenue generation, an investor can advance the possibility that the rocket will achieve escape velocity and - let's all hold our breath - orbit. Remember, the fuel is not the technology, product or service that the company offers - it is revenue.

Use of time: I recently had drinks with an investor who had just visited the offices of one of his 'sick puppies'. What struck him the most was that the entire staff - including the sales and business development people - was in the office. A conversation with the CEO had made him feel even worse. The CEO was not concerned - and here was the worst part - did not see that sales was his responsibility. It had been delegated.

Now, I will reveal a prejudice here. For my money, in a start-up the only CEOs worth paying are ones that act as the chief business development and sales leader of the team. A CEO who either cannot or will not sell isn't worth a bucket of spit.

Investors need to set and enforce metrics that insure that the time paid for - the team - is being used affectively, aggressively and in a well-focused manner. Overly delicate CEOs who think that selling is beneath them, business development types who see selling as something that the troops do after they make the initial contact and sales people who think they can do their job from an office need to be taken out behind the woodshed and have the world explained to them. The principle purpose of a start-up revolves around sales and the selling process. Everything else pales next to revenue generation.

- Never invest in a company headed by a CEO who either cannot or will not sell - good start-up CEOs are relentless and effective sales people.

- Never invest in a start-up that has a business development person and a sales team - unless you can first cleave away the business development type - it is all about sales.

- Never accept results that are driven by either the aversion or inability to close deals - sure, generating revenue is hard but failure to master and overcome those difficulties is a sure prescription for failure.

- Always show a preference of investment opportunities with a team that has already begun to generate revenues - there is nothing wrong with the second stage providing lift along with the boosters.

- Always move decisively when sales is not generating acceptable results -

if these guys can't get it done, find
some others who can.

Applying the Metrics

Reporting: From the paragraphs above, it should be clear that I am advocating a relatively compact and focused set of initial metrics. You should not be measuring everything or many things that do not matter. Once you have settled on the metrics, it is important to require regular and concise reporting. The most effective way of tracking progress is through a relatively frequent series of investor briefings. The agenda for these briefings should track the metrics.

Interrogating: It is important to verify reported results. A 'veracity test' will keep the management team from 'fudging' the results. Aside from the clear benefit of verification, the requirements for confirmation of results will help to establish a culture of transparency within the company. It will also reinforce the idea that management is accountable for the result they generate not the results they dress up to make themselves look good. As an old friend used to say, "It is what it is. Calling it by another name is just plain foolish. Deceiving others is deceiving yourself - and you owe yourself more respect than that."

The best way to verify is to bypass the management that has presented the results and visit with the keepers of the records. The controller or bookkeeper is often a good source. A chat with the person handling accounts receivable can yield good information. Visiting with the people who are in direct contact with customers will generate a lot of useful information. Finally, visiting with selected customers can help fill in the background for the reported progress.

I once worked with a CEO who took umbrage at my constant poking around after the investor - that is until I uncovered a problem that threatened the entire company. It was an innocent mistake - an oversight in underestimating the financial resources needed to bridge the time between receipt of a purchase order and receipt of the funds from the customer. Having saved the company from a financial crisis, the CEO offered that I could poke around as much as I liked.

CEOs who object to close oversight - who are secretive and withhold information that might make them look more human than their ego allows - whose mental picture of the world is 'me against them' - need to be avoided like the plague. In truth, that is exactly what they are. Business is a team undertaking. To succeed requires optimal use of all resources - an aggressive elimination of blind spots and other foolishnesses - and a subordination of ego to the greater good of the company. CEOs that are incapable of understanding this may be very good at the business of the business but will most often be failures at the business of business.

Adjusting: Measuring must lead to modifications. The purpose of metrics is to provide a solid basis for sensible adjustments to the existing arrangements. The formulae 'if this, then that' is what needs to operate. This means that the nature and calculation of the adjustments needs to be agreed on before hand - in the definitive agreement that is signed prior to the investment being made.

Two of the adjustments near and dear to the heart of any CEO is the recalculation of equity ownership and the determination of the levels of compensation. Both of these formulae need to be clearly defined in the definitive agreement. The more 'mechanical' the calculation is the better drawn the agreement. Ideally, the definitive agreement will anticipate all possible disagreements. Here, ideally is the operative word. In practice, a well-designed conflict resolution scheme is critical to resolving such disagreements. Remember, the only time metrics become a problem is then performance is less than projected. Management that was expecting to increase significantly their equity stake and compensation levels based on projected results may find it difficult to come to terms with the fact that they failed to achieve those results. Without an effective conflict resolution program in place, the 'blame game' will flourish - and that is best avoided for nothing good ever comes from it.

Dealing with the Results: Metrics are useless unless they are tied to results and the responses to those results. They should not only be the codified basis of an understanding between you and your investors. They should also provide an automatic adjustment to new realities. If they only result in a general agreement that 'expectations were not met' both you and the investors will end up in one or more of the dismal swamps described above.

If you do not meet expectation, your compensation and ownership should be adjusted downwards. If, on the other hand, you exceed expectations your compensation and ownership should be adjusted upwards.

An essential part of developing and following good metrics is the 'adult conversations' that take place when what was expected turns into what is known. A professional investor will not only insist on this arrangement but will be happy to see you earn more by your success.

Evolving the Metrics: Finally, metrics should evolve as the company grows. I do not mean to suggest that failure to meet expectations should result in a lowering of expectations. I mean that new metrics will be required as the company matures. Your relationship with your investors should allow for this.

Making Metrics Work

Making metrics work begins with the development of metrics for the metrics. This is not a cute word play - it is the essence of good management. Whenever you are managing a set of metrics, you should ask yourself:

Are they clear and concise? Do the metrics define concisely what they are measuring?

Do they track the measurable? 'Soft' metrics pave the road to disaster. The kind of Age of Aquarius - touchy-feely - stuff that can creep into management may have a purpose in other areas but it is destructive when it comes to tracking progress towards increasing shareholder value.

Are we measuring tangible results? Investors should proactively set metrics that tie into their objectives as investors. As an example, tracking the pipeline may be useful for good management but revenue generation that should be the focus of metrics.

Do the metrics and the results they measure have an impact on the company and management team? Do they provide a means to adjust compensation and equity ownership?

Are the metrics useful in the review process? Investors should regularly conduct performance reviews. The metrics should provide a solid and mutually agreed on basis for those reviews.

Have the metrics been agreed on prior to the investment? This is one area where angel investors fail to protect their own interests. The term sheet should contain a provision calling for agreement on metrics prior to any funds being transfers.

Have you proved for a resolution of conflict? In an ideal world, metrics should be so clearly defined and the performance review process described in such detail that alternate interpretations are not possible. However, where compensation and equity interests come in, disagreements occur. It is important to agree on the mechanism for resolving these differences of opinion before any funds are transferred.

In Summary

Starting with paragraph one: Some years back a friend and mentor taught me the 'dangers of the *casual of course*'. I was learning the ropes on Wall Street and early in one of my first transactions, he came on board as an advisor to provide adult supervision. During our second review meeting he challenged me for 'leaping over' ground that should be carefully covered and assuming that nothing would be lost by doing so.

After some prodding, and more than a small dose of straight talk, I began to see what he was getting at. The casual of course is dangerous indeed and the reasons that it occurs is even more dangerous. The underlying drivers of my tendencies to leap right to the structuring of this particular deal was a combination of conflict aversion, lack of confidence and a hesitancy rooted in a reflexively assumed subordinate position.

It took me more than that one deal to work through that load of baggage. First, I had to recognize that tension can be therapeutic and sometimes the only way to reach the levels of understanding and agreement to 'knock the rough edges off an agreement and put it into winning form'. Second, I had to accept that I had a responsibility that came with my role - one that, if I did not meet it, could cost many people a lot of money. It didn't make any difference that others at the table had more experience that I did - I had to meet my responsibilities best as I could and not let anybody interfere with my meeting them. When it came to the deal structure, 'I was the man'. That was the third thing I had to learn. All the other parties at the table would prefer an easier arrangement than I needed to insist on. It was my job to insist - to make sure that the interests were aligned and the interests of my constituency - the investors - were not harmed or subordinated.

Jim's massage was simple - "*start with paragraph one and don't assume anything. Avoid the casual of-courses*".

- Of course these guys can build a business
- Of course their technology is sound and meets a strongly felt need
- Of course there are no disruptive technologies coming down the pike - if there were, these guys would be aware of them
- Of course they will monetize the value proposition
- Of course my role is to merely provide the funding and sit back to collect the rewards
- Of course the management team's contribution is worth more than mine and I should be happy with a minority interest based on a valuation which could not possibly be validated by any measure of market-

determined value

I hope you get the idea. I have hundreds more that I have listened to over the years but, if the point is not taken based on the list above, it is unlikely that more will help much. The suggestion here is that - even if it causes conflict and risks getting the deal - it is important that these and other questions be answered in a way that survives the cold light of day.

When all is said and done, the relationship between you and your investors is a combining of two different world views. They are in it for a return on their investment. You are in it to build a company and to reap the benefits of having done that. Find a common ground - reach a clear understanding - treat their perspective with respect and honor their objectives.

If you want to learn more about dealing with angel investors and how I can help you get funded, send me an e-mail and we will arrange a time for a free consultation.

Venture Capitalists

Introduction

The Money Chase has been the death of many good companies. There are a range of reasons why this is so. Some companies simply do not deserve funding - they are not an attractive investment opportunity. Others embark on the money chase too early. They haven't established the business base to justify funding. Still others are run by people who seem to like the money chase better than running the business. All of these reasons and more make embarking on the search for venture funding a perilous business which risks your company and all it may become.

Over the years, I have worked with a large number of companies and management teams that have sailed these choppy seas. I've written this book to let you in on some of the knowledge - sometimes hard won - that I have accumulated.

If you have been successful in building your company to a certain stage, you will be tempted to search for the financial resources that will allow you to take it to the next level. The question is not if but how you will pursue that funding; whether you will adequately understand the new world that you enter when you begin to talk to angel investors and venture capitalists.

The money chase is a high-speed race through a darkened labyrinth that has many blind alleys and circular paths. It is easy to get lost in that labyrinth. The judges are unforgiving of amateurs and their blunders.

The idea of being judged by potential investors is often an uncomfortable one for founders. That has always been strange to me because they are constantly being judged by their customers, team members and stakeholders. But investors seem to present a particular challenge. I suspect it is because of the 'mercenary' vision that investors can bring to the table. They are providing funding and are looking for a major return on that investment. The perspective is so tightly focused that founders, who have a more holistic vision of their company, can feel threatened or offended by such an opportunistic approach.

If the goal is getting funded - as opposed to ineffectively grousing about how unfair the world is and how narrow minded investors are - then founders need to understand the money chase from the investor's point of view. Helping you do the latter is one of the major objectives of this book.

Fred Got Funded – And He Hasn't Had a Good Day Since

Most entrepreneurs dream of the day that the investor's check clears and they have the funding to grow their business. It is a day that they struggle to achieve. Most put in long hours of preparation. They polish and re-polish their elevator speech and dog-and-pony show. The slide stack is revised and re-revised. The diligent ones even look to their own performance and appearance during the presentations to find ways to improve results and finally greet that sunrise on funding day.

Fred was one of those types. He led his team on a magnificent money chase. Over the course of about six months, they probably made two dozen presentations before finding an angel investor willing to write a check. They went into that last meeting in full stride. Fred and his team had honed their presentation skills to a fine point. They had developed effective responses to all the important questions and were able to, easily and professionally, respond to every question. Fred's team was the epitome of persuasiveness. In the broad scheme of things, they only had one weakness – Fred's business idea was not ready for prime time. They had not done the spade work to mature the business model – particularly the revenue model.

The Short Honeymoon

The first months after funding were euphoric for both Fred's team and the angel investor who had funded the company. Sure, there were some rough spots; the investor seemed more intrusive than Fred had anticipated and customers were not responding to the value proposition as anticipated. "*But that is just the fog of a startup,*" Fred observed. The team was working out how to interact with the investor. The investor was working out how to work with Fred's team. Everything would work out in the end.

One major bump in the road did cause Fred some concern. The investor was much more focused on the numbers than Fred had anticipated. He seemed to see the company in terms of spreadsheets and constantly pressured the financial person on the team to come up with more and more sophisticated analysis of the numbers. It finally got so bad that the controller quit. The first member of the team left after only two months. "*Good riddance*", was the investor's response, "*I have somebody who will do a far better job.*" When Fred attempted to recruit a new financial member for his team, he got a shock. The investor showed him that the funding agreement required investor approval for major hires and the investor would only approve his anointed candidate. For Fred, the question became "*who is running this company?*" For the investor, the statement was "*I am*".

The Straw …

While the struggle over control was going on, something else became clear. Fred and his team had spent so much energy and focus on perfecting their investor presentation that they had neglected to refine and test their business model. Over the six months prior to funding Fred had spent almost all of his time chasing money. He had neglected the developing contacts with potential customers. As more and more of his team were drawn into the money chase, they ceased to evolve their understanding to the business and its value proposition. They became very good at selling what they had – but what they had was not sufficient to become a profitable business.

That straw that broke the camel's back was the need for the team to go back to the drawing boards and redesign the value proposition. Instead of using the funding to establish a market position, the team drew salaries and revamped the business plan. As the bank balance diminished the tension between the investor and Fred's team increased. Eventually, things erupted into open warfare. The investor accused Fred and his team of conning him into investing in a poorly formed and tested idea. Fred defended himself and his team. They were doing the best they could under the circumstances. The investor's intrusive tendencies had caused a drop in morale. The new financial person was not fitting into the team. Some of the key team members were thinking of leaving.

May I Have the Mediator Please?

There is often very little to do in such situations but try to get the parties separated. Tragic experiences are sometimes best left behind and all parties are better off if they can lick their wounds and move on. I was asked to intervene in this situation by the investor. Even though the investor suggested my involvement, Fred welcomed it. From his point of view, there had to be some relief no matter what the source. Things were falling apart. It did not take long for me to present initial findings:

The focus on the money chase and then the use of the funding had been very bad for Fred's team. They lost their entrepreneurial edge. Instead of thinking how to build a business – of new ways to implement on a shoestring – they had focused on the need to convince an investor to write a check. Their tendency to think creatively and to focus on innovating their space was substantially reduced and eventually virtually eliminated by the pressures of the money chase.

Fred's team came to think of their most

important audience as the investor instead of their base of potential customers. They spent a lot of time trying to figure out how to make the company attractive to investors and not nearly as much time trying to figure out how to make the company's value proposition attractive to potential customers. The result was that they won the battle but were in danger of losing the war.

The investor had substantially overstepped his prerogatives and had acted as a 'shadow CEO'. His passion for financial analysis had overridden prudence. After writing the check, he should have reduced his footprint and became much less of a distraction. In other words, he should have let Fred and his team gets about the business of building a business. He was, after all, only an investor and not a member of the management team. But that did not happen. Instead, he became a major distraction and eventually destabilized Fred's team.

Once the focus shifted to restructuring the value proposition, the investor found himself in the middle of a re-development process. The team was doing what they should have done before embarking on the money chase – they were trying to figure out how to build a business out of their vision. But, this was not what the investor signed on for. He expected that this work would have been done before funding. He had a point, but he was also culpable as a facilitator of an inadequate process. He invested before it was prudent to do so

Facing Reality Often Means Looking in the Mirror

There were no smiles in the room after I had presented my findings. Both the investor and Fred's team had major roles in creating the train wreck. The question was, "*now what do we do?*" That was going to be the hard part because there were no easy or painless solutions.

"*Look,*" I said, "*there are only a few ways forward that make any sense. The first is to put the company out of its misery; declare bankruptcy and close it down. You can then work out who owes whom what. The second is to renegotiate your understanding and find a new way forward. That would require both sides to find reasons for doing so. I would be glad to facilitate that process but would insist on certain undertakings from both sides beforehand. The third option is to reach an agreement that allows you to go your separate ways without closing the company. That would involve the management team 'buying out' the investor. It is not possible that the investor could be made whole if that means returning the funds advanced. But there may be alternative arrangements that would make sense.*"

It took a couple of days for both sides to sort out their options and preferences but they finally decided on the third way forward. We set about negotiating the terms of an amicable separation. But that is a story for another time. For now, the lesson I want to highlight is -

Be careful what you wish for. Wishing and having are two very different things.

Investors Are Human Too

I recently sat in on a gab fest of entrepreneurs and wannabee entrepreneurs. The subject of investors and how best to approach them came up and I was taken aback by what I heard. If you listened to these guys investors were stupid, arrogant, greedy, short-sighted, overbearing, intrusive, and difficult to deal with and distinctly neither a recognized nor welcomed part of the human race. Investors were the scourge of the business world and responsible for most of the failures in it. What set me back were the obvious questions:

"OK, if these people are this way, why would you have anything to do with them?"
"If these people knew how little you thought of them, why would they ever consider investing with you?"

Uncharacteristically, I held my questions and decided to ask the 'other side' what they thought about the conversation. So I organized an informal session of investors and put the question to them. After I had described the 'bitching gaggle' and named the most prominent participants, here is a bit of what they offered:

"Yeah, we know about these types. The grapevine brings us their names and we don't take them or their proposals seriously."

"These guys are so busy ratifying their own provincial perspective that they never see the process from ours. Most of them think they can simply present a good business plan to strangers and get a commitment on the spot. They treat us like an ATM"
"They are only one kind that I see ... the majority, to be sure, but not the only kind. Some – the very best of them – learn that they need to get to know us and let us get to know them. They approach us as serious people and work to establish a relationship based on trust and mutual respect."

The last comment echoed something that I have been telling founders for years. "You need to start a year or more in advance to establish relationships with potential investors before attempting to raise capital from them." Most investors respond professionally to this possibility; that is to say, they either pursue or turn away from such approaches depending on how well the founders and their value proposition resonates with the investor's interest. This process takes intelligence, sound judgment, planning and perseverance. The founder who misses the boat tends to have the ATM perspective. They wait until it is far too late to begin the process of building relationships with investors. By that time, their company can't wait for a year to raise the capital it needs.

The unavoidable fact is that investors are humans focused on a human purpose. And, as such, they are not, by definition, stupid, arrogant, greedy, short-sighted, overbearing, intrusive or difficult to deal with. They typically won't invest unless they have direct or indirect relationships with founders and companies. Every investor has many investment opportunities. The ones they invest in are companies they know more about than they learn from an elevator pitch or a business plan.

Through all the companies I founded and companies I have worked with, I have never known one to successfully raise capital from total strangers. Typically, the investor had a relationship over a significant period of time with a member of the founding team. The relationship was based on trust and experience. In other words, those founders who were successful in raising capital most often saw investors in positive, rather than negative, lights.

To summarize, according to my informal focus group, the key to successfully raising capital from investors is to establish a relationship with them so that the investors can get to know the founders, their business ideas and the kinds of business people they really are. If the relationship develops into a good fit, these investors become a champion to other investors.

Now let's return to the group. I wanted to see if the investors that I had gathered had any opinions as to why certain founders saw them is such negative lights and held them in such low esteem. *"OK guys, what drives these types to think so poorly of the very people they need to help their business grow?"* Here is some of what they offered:

"I see it as a form of immaturity. These are essentially angry children. Many of them puff up their chest, proclaim a long and successful career (such pretensions seldom survive even a cursory diligence) and pontificate on things they know little or nothing about."

"It is the uninformed showing the unwilling how to do the unnecessary. These people are really nobodies parading as somebody. They do a lot of damage to the chances of other founders. By the time they begin to think this way, they are not founders anymore; just proselytizers."

"It's just background noise mostly. But there is some benefit. We tend to keep close track of those who pontificate in such a manner and politely decline to engage with them in any way. The internet is such a great source of information. I once was approached by a founder who pitched me an interesting idea. I Goggled him and found lots of derogatory comments he had made about how stupid and destructive investors were. Needless to say, I did not pursue discussions with him."

"Who in their right mind would do business with somebody who thinks you are an idiot?"

I keep a cartoon on my desk. It is from the Simpsons TV show. It is called "old man yells at cloud". I am amazed at how young some of these old men are."

I suppose that my logical next step would have been to re-gather the group of founders and discuss my experience with the investors. But I long ago lost the passion for kamikaze raids on vacant lots. So, instead of wading into the fray, I have decided to put these thoughts down and float them out into the clouds.

Investors are people too and like all people they respond better to others who both understand and have compassion for their chosen role in life.

Venture Capital – The First Meeting

You seldom get a second chance to make a first impression. This is a very important lesson when it comes to meeting with venture capitalists.

~~~~~~~~~~~~~~~~~~~~

I do a lot of work with companies seeking financing. Whether it is a first round or follow-on, funding for further research and development or marketing and branding efforts, equity or debt financing, a start-up or mid-market company or financing to prepare for acquisition by a strategic buyer, there are strategies which can significantly improve the prospects for success. In this chapter I want to focus on preparations for and managing the initial meeting with a venture capitalist.

First meeting with venture capitalists presents multiple challenges. Many of these challenges are best addressed with guidance from an experienced professional. There is simply no substitute for having been through the process successfully multiple times. Over the years, and as a result of working with a large number of companies, I have developed a 'first meeting' checklist. Here are a few of the items on it:

Pre-screen the funds you approach: Focus

on funds which understand and have a preference for investing in your space and your phase (seed, early-stage, etc.). Most venture capitalists make their list of portfolio companies available on their website. That makes it easy to identify those who prefer to invest in your stage, industry and technology. But identifying the fund is not enough. You need to identify the partner who will be the most interested in your presentation.

The rifle is better than the shotgun: Avoid 'wallpapering the world'. It is certainly a good idea to approach a small number of potential investors at the same time. But you do not want to give the impression that you are shopping your company on the street. Also, be careful not to get yourself into an 'auction' frame of mind before you actually have more than one serious bidder.

Avoid presenting to investors who lack a general understanding of your space: I have sat in on presentations by companies whose value proposition was so alien to the focus of the venture fund that I began to wonder if the presenters had not entered the wrong door along the hallway and should be presenting to one of the other venture funds in the building. If your value proposition and technologies are completely foreign to the fund's investment strategy the meeting will be over early on.

Be clear on why you want to raise venture

capital: This is one of those 'of course' questions that sometime slips through the cracks. You should be able to communicate not only why you are seeking venture financing but also why this particular form of financing rather than any of a wide range of options is most suitable. Your explanation needs to be reasonable and clearly well thought out. You also must make a strong case for the amount you are seeking and how you need it funded (i.e.: if you need it all up front or are willing to take it in tranches based on milestones).

Red-team your presentation mercilessly: One of the most important contributions that I make is through arranging red-teaming sessions. I bring together individuals with expertise in the technology and combine them with experienced venture fund managers. The client is instructed to approach these meetings as if they were a session with venture fund principals. As practice sessions, these meetings go a long way to refine and streamline the presentation and can radically improve the probabilities of success.

Highlight your relevant past experience: Many presenters overlook the fact that their credibility is as much on the line during this initial meeting as the viability of the product/ service offering. Yes, the venture capitalist is highly interested in your value proposition. Yes, they will focus on the potential for monetizing that value proposition. But they will also be deciding whether you and your team are capable of implementing. One way to help them do this is to talk about why your past experience and accomplishments make you a good candidate to exploit the opportunity.

Be on time: An old girlfriend used to say that there were two kinds of guys she just couldn't stand – those that showed up early and eager and those that were late and useless. Plan the logistics carefully and make sure that you reliably arrive at the site of the meeting five to ten minutes before hand. Be sure that your team is assembled before hand – and make sure that somebody puts a leash on the one team member who is always late. The insult of wasting somebody's time is one of the worst that you can manage. It will become clear immediately to the people who you are meeting that you don't respect them or their time. How likely are you to succeed when starting off with such an unnecessary liability?

Manage the meeting: Time management is critical in the first session. Keep the first 1/3 of the meeting focused on your presentation. That means that questions which might come up should be postponed to after the end of the presentation if at all possible. If you are successful in doing this, you will end up with the second 1/3 of the meeting for discussions.

Now I know what you're thinking – that's only 2/3 – what happened to the other 1/3? Well take it from someone who has been through a lot of these sessions, if you're meeting is scheduled for an hour it will most likely, after adjustments for people being late, cell phones ringing, interruptions of an amazing variety and the general conspiracy against order, turn out to be more like forty minutes. Manage the meeting and your time under the assumption that that's all the time that you are going to have. If the fates don't conspire against you, the extra twenty minutes will be pure bonus.

If you are not well prepared and focused, the venture capitalist will get impatient and take over the pace of the meeting. Many VCs will deliberately jump in with questions and requests which may be on Slide 12, while you are still presenting Slide 4. Here is a great tip: structure the presentation so that all the most important information is in the first few slides.

In an important way, clock management is a test of your ability to manage a process under pressure. One VC recently told me "*In our case, if we schedule a meeting for 90 minutes, we terminate it after 90 minutes, even if the entrepreneur is in the middle of a PowerPoint slide.*"

Layout your value proposition at the outset: You need to present your value proposition within the first five minutes of the meeting.

By that I mean a presentation which highlights the problems that the company's solutions are designed to address, the advantages of those solutions over competing ones, the clientele for which these advantages will be important and a clear statement of how you intend to monetize the value proposition – all within the first five minutes.

I have watched entrepreneurs spend fifteen or twenty minutes getting ready to deliver their value proposition punch line. The problem with this approach is that they lost the attention of their audience long before they got to the most important part of the presentation. One VC suggested the following: "The way I like to see this presented is: Slide 2 is "The Pain" and Slide 3 is "The Cure."

Manage the level of detail: Remember that the initial meeting is designed to give the venture capitalist a first brush description of your company and team. Approach the meeting as an executive summary of the chapters that may follow – or as a first paragraph designed to draw the readers in and make them want to read on. You need to hit the high points and emphasize your strengths – outline your intended responses to important challenges. Avoid the 'And now for the first of 45 slides ..." approach – keep it down to ten or twelve summary level slides. Brief the venture capitalist; don't bury them in an avalanche of detail.

But don't oversimplify your value proposition: Solutions to complex problems are most often complex. If this is the case with your company, it is important to communicate your understanding of that complexity and how your solutions will reduce its effects to manageable levels. Red–teaming with an outside group of experts can be particularly helpful in refining this type of presentation.

For a first meeting, there is a delicate balance between over-simplification on the one hand and drowning the audience in a sea of details on the other. You need to design your presentation to adequately describe levels of complexity while making sure that the presentation can still be completed (and comprehended) within the time available. It is always good to leave them wanting more.

Turn off your cell phone: This is one of those prescriptions that one would think would be unnecessary. But I have sat through too many luncheon events with a moderator who begins by asking everybody to turn off their phone only to have the keynote speaker interrupted mid-sentence by some moron's custom ring tones. Do yourself a favor. Before you go into the meeting turn off your cell phone. If you can't trust yourself to do that, leave it in the car. According to one VC, "*Personally, I tune out totally the entrepreneur whose phone has rung. I may miss some good deals this way, but I don't want to be involved with anyone who has no respect for me."*

Situational understanding is a key: This is one of the areas where working with a very experienced advocate can yield huge benefits. Situational dynamics is the awareness of what is going on around you – and an initial meeting with a venture capitalist is indeed a complex process. It is important that you understand what is going on within the frame of reference of the venture capitalist. Make sure that you understand what is at stake at each stage, the most likely outcomes, which of them will lead to a next step and what that next step is likely to be.

It is their process that you are involved in not yours: One of the toughest things to remember is that you are a guest in the venture capitalists house (even if the presentation takes place in your conference room) and engaged in a ritual process which has been designed and is enforced by the occupant. Many entrepreneurs get used to getting their own way by force of will. Some believe that a forceful presentation coupled with an insistence on a positive result will succeed. Both of these strategies are inherently flawed. The decision-making process within a venture fund is most often collegiate and often highly ritualized and, although the individual you are meeting with may have a major say, investment decisions are generally made after a collaborative process – most of which occurs outside of the experience of the entrepreneur.

Every step of the way with a VC has as its primary goal to get to the next step: Many entrepreneurs enter an initial meeting with a burning desire to get through the process and be funded as soon as possible. As a result they try to provide the entire range of diligence requirements within the boundaries of one meeting. The dominant purpose of an initial meeting with a venture capitalist is to decide whether there is going to be a second meeting. In order to decide this, the VC is going to need enough basic information to decide whether to commit resources to doing further diligence. In fact, I consistently tell clients that the only thing you should be looking for as a result of the initial meeting is a request for next meeting. Forget about the platitudes and how nice this person is being to you – how enthralled they seem with your technologies. The only thing that matters is that they want to see you again.

Be prepared for the obvious questions: One of the great benefits of red-teaming is that these questions are surfaced and dealt with during these practice sessions. I can't tell you how many times I have sat in on presentations that have gone wrong very quickly simply because the presenters did not have these responses rehearsed. In one case, the business plan included projections of operating results which started in January. The presentation was done in April. One of the venture capitalists observed that, if the company was on target, they should have a year to date revenue of X dollars. Of course they didn't and the meeting was purely perfunctory thereafter. Another entrepreneur was asked a rather standard question "Who are your principal competitors?" He glibly responded, "We are unique and nobody does what we do." The venture capitalist was a pro in their space and casually reeled off a list of at least a dozen companies that competed either directly or indirectly. As before, the meeting was over and the rest was just professional courtesy to the person who had sponsored them.

Present with passion: There is a fine line between presenting with passion and inappropriate (messianic) exuberance. You need to communicate that this is a business that you passionately believe in and have committed to. The venture capitalist needs to come away with the feeling that you will do what is necessary to make the company a success. VCs generally don't like to invest with entrepreneurs who are out to 'change the world as we know it'. Recent experience has graphically demonstrated the risks that this approach can entail. They invest with teams who understand how their advantages can be turned into a viable business – and how to make money for the investors along the way.

Establish credibility: Once a venture capitalist has come to the conclusion that your value proposition is a good one his/her attention will then turn to another question which often does not occur to entrepreneurs. "*OK, these guys have a good idea but are they the team to make it happen?*" Most venture capitalists will tell you that if they face the choice between investing in an A-level idea with a C-level team on the one hand or a C-level idea with an A-level team, the A-level team will always get their vote. Assume that, if they are involved in the space, they will have seen others with similar approaches. Your team may be the most important differentiator. The credibility you establish in the first meeting may be your best asset.

Speak part of the time from the point of view of the customer: "*Amateurs have markets while professionals have clients.*" Those words are tattooed on the inside of many venture capitalists' eyelids. Make sure that you spend part of your presentation talking about your company from the perspective of your clients. And stay away from the 'this is a billion dollar space and if we can get just 1% …' crap. It is the kiss of death for presentations to VCs and a clear indication that an amateur is presenting.

Remember that the decision is theirs and

not yours: You are providing information. The venture capitalist will decide whether or not they are interested in arranging a follow-up meeting. That is their decision not yours and most likely he/she will want to make it after thinking about your presentation and discussing it with their partners. Your deliverable in this first meeting is a concise description of your company, senior team, value proposition, competitive advantages and the purpose to which you are intending to use the proceeds of an investment. Accomplish those goals, ask for an estimated schedule for their response (when are you likely to hear from them) and feedback as to whether you accomplish them (how well you did in presenting). Finally, indicate that you are prepared to respond if the venture capitalist decides they want to go to the next level.

And don't call or e-mail the VC after the meeting except to thank them for the time and attention that they gave you. Pestering will not improve your chances – if they have something to say to you, they will initiate the contact.

Don't take 'Not Interested' as a condemnation: A rejection can carry a number of meanings. It may simply be a reflection that the interests of the venture fund are not well aligned with your company. The fund may be fully invested in your space and want to diversify. Or they may have decided that you are not the person to exploit the opportunity. But a rejection is a matter of judgment by an individual fund not a demonstration of truth. Learn from your experience, process the feedback that you are able to get and work to improve your presentation – sharpen your message. Then get back out there and present to another fund. Persistence cannot carry a poor cause to victory – but timidity and lack of persistence can condemn a good one to a premature extinction.

Like most journeys into the unknown, an efficient search for venture funding is best done under the guidance of an experienced professional. Sure, you can go it alone – but time and tide will tend to work against you. Most professionals will work with you for a small retainer – with most of their compensation coming through a success fee and an accumulation of equity in the company. You would do well to follow the example of the ship's captain who, upon bringing his charge safely to the mouth of the harbor, acquires the services of a harbor pilot in order to arrive safely and quickly at the quay.

Presenting to Early Stage Venture Capitalists - A Few Things to Remember

Here are some suggestions that will help you better manage your meetings with investors. They are garnered from years of experience and many meetings. Following them will improve the results and increase the chances of a favorable outcome.

~~~~~~~~~~~~~~~~~~~~

The most the important difference is that early stage investors have to deal with a class of uncertainties that are much the better quantified in the later stages of a company's growth. Their attitude towards risk aversion and the focus of their diligence can be quite different. Additionally, because there are no significant 'corporate tracks in the snow', these investors very often have to make 'leaps of faith' based on their gut feel.

In this chapter, I want to focus on some of the threshold questions that are almost always on the checklist of every early stage investor. Many of these issues will seem logical to founders but often the logic they see in them is not the logic that the investor applies.

Investment Focus: Most early stage investors specialize in a relatively narrow range of areas. They rely on their experience and expertise in these spaces to help them avoid major missteps and to identify those opportunities for major gains. For instance, I know of one very substantial group of angel investors that strongly prefers information sciences and the life sciences. Given this focus it makes little sense to present a consumer goods company to them. But as any early stage investor will tell you this 'myth of fingerprints' happens all the time.

Often the investor's web site will help identify investment preferences. But sometimes even the portfolios which are listed can mask decisions which the group has made. For instance, they may have historically had a preference for investment in a particular space but now, with a significant portion of their total deployed capital involved in that space, may have decided that enough is enough – that they need to diversify. Considerably more current intelligence is required to make sure that a team is presenting appropriately.

Let's assume that the founders have done their homework or employed an experienced and well-connected professional to help them target the right investment groups. Now they have a list of potential investors who are likely to listen with interest. But with that, the challenge has only begun. You may be talking to the right people but you may be saying the wrong things to them. So in that spirit, here are a few areas that are going to be of particular interest to the early stage investor.

The Founding Team: The days when the technology alone was enough to guarantee funding are long gone. In fact most early stage investors will focus on the founding team before they focus on the technology. This tends to be true for two reasons. The first is that recent experience has led them to realize that an early stage investment is first and foremost an investment in people. From their point of view, the management team needs to consist of very experienced individuals who can credibly execute the business plan being presented. Team members need to be able to modify the plan on the run and be battle tested in the chaos that always accompanies a start-up. They need to be the kinds of people who see their company's growth in terms of critical yet achievable milestones to the next stage of funding.

This last point needs to be clearly understood by the founders. An early stage investor's horizon extends to the next stage of funding. This event constitutes their first opportunity to either cash out or establish an increased evaluation for their investment.

Certainly investors will want to make sure that the team has a CEO that can lead the company through its early stages. They will also want to see significant experience in important skill areas. All of this can lead the founders to think that their horizons and those of the investors are coterminous. This is a serious mistake. Investors want to see a team which is passionately committed to building the company into a dominating player in its space. But they see themselves as only being a long for part of that ride. Their threshold question is *"Are these guys going to make a good, relatively short-term and highly profitable investment for me?"*

The Market: I recently heard an early stage investors say that the best decision making process for their group was anti-democratic. By that, she meant that when everybody in the group was ready to vote 'yes' on a particular investment opportunity it was probably not a good idea to make the investment. The most successful investments that her group had made were advanced and defended by one or two of her partners with the investment being made over the reservations of the rest.

Early stage investors by their nature prefer opportunities which are disruptive to existing technologies. They look for a 'big idea' in a relatively small but rapidly expanding market. They don't tend to be attracted to marginal improvements which yield marginal returns. They're in the business of betting on the nature of the next new world.

These investors tend to react negatively to certain mistakes by founders. Here is one quick example that might help illuminate this point. Although it happens less frequently these days many teams approach the question of the market for their product or services by estimating the demand on a global or national basis and then projecting a market penetration of 1% or 2%. The relevant section of the business plan would end with a statement something like if 'we only get X-percent of the total market, we will have a billion dollar company'. But these days investors tend not to buy that logic. In fact they often see it as an indication of a lack of professionalism within the venture team. As one friend and experienced investor is fond of saying "amateurs have markets while professionals have customers".

So, for these investors, the relative attractiveness of an investment opportunity turns on the attractiveness of the market combined with the ability of the team to implement. The size and growth rates within the market are important metrics. Investors also tend to focus on the industry structure, barriers to entry, customer switching costs, competitive landscape, behavior of incumbents, etc. Small markets seldom deliver the opportunity to build big companies. But neither do big, well established markets heavily populated by close-variation competition.

Remember when it comes to early stage investors 'disruptive' is an important word. Ideally the product or service being offered should be disruptive and unique. It should address a problem or meet a need in a truly innovative way and which establishes a clear and sustainable competitive advantage over presently existing solutions.

The Business Model: The model is the means by which the team explains how it intends to develop profitable, sustainable business. But there are a few more characteristics of the model which will draw the attention of early stage investors.

Most angel investors are going to want to see major impacts from the capitol they provide. They tend to prefer businesses and business models that are not capital intensive. They're also attracted to businesses with high and sustainable gross margins. The combination of these two factors within a high growth market that can support a high, internally sustainable growth rate is the holy grail of early stage investors.

Entrepreneurs need to be incredibly parsimonious – conserving scarce resources while generating huge effects when they are deployed. It is important to remember that most early stage investors will have seen many attempts to implement similar business models. They will have seen teams fritter away resources ineffectively. They will not want to see their invested capital suffer the same fate.

Most of these investors see a business plan as a dynamic undertaking. The pristine logic of it is not nearly as important to them as the plans for implementation. Start-ups will go through very chaotic stages on their way to stability. Success in navigating these challenges will require a team which is agile and willing to completely a remake the business plan if circumstances conspire against the original approach. Investors become very leery if they suspect that a team is adopting an "our way or the highway" approach. In all early stage ventures, all business planning is provisional.

The Competition: This is one of those areas where many teams really drop the ball. If they are presenting to investors who have historically indicated a preference for investing in their space, they're going to find themselves in front of professionals who may have a far more thorough going understanding of the competitive landscape. These investors may have seen many variations on the theme that the team is presenting. They may be familiar with alternative approaches to structuring and delivering a value proposition. They may even have seen similar proposals get funded and fail. Presenting teams would do well to keep this in mind and avoid either being dismissive of the competition or understating its potency.

The management team needs to display a mastery of the competitive landscape and understand both its present and future direct and indirect competitors. Their understanding should be based on extensive research and extended personal experience in the space. The team needs to establish a value proposition that gives it an advantage over the competition. But they also need to have a firm grasp on how that advantage is going to be sustainable.

The Exit Strategy: This is another one of those areas where teams need to operate on assumptions which clash with the objectives of the early stage investor. The liquidity event for the angel investor is almost never a liquidity event for the founders. The investors are interested in teams that can credibly build a company that will thrive and attract additional investment. Most of them will want to exit before the company's liquidity event.

Early stage investors are in the business of deploying capital for a relatively short period of time and realizing significant gains through a near-term liquidity event which returns all or most of their capital. They will be happy to hear that the team has successfully built annual revenues of $200,000,000.00 and that the company has been acquired by a major public company – or that it has successfully arranged an IPO.

In fact most will tell you that they favor management teams that have the 'company building' mindset versus the 'build-it to flip it' approach. But they expect to cash out early on and well before the company's liquidity event. They have other early stage investments to make.

How to Get Ready to Present: Founders need to realize that investors think about their company in a completely different way than they do. Their request for funding needs to be presented within the investors' frame of reference. Arranging the first round of investment is difficult enough without having it made more difficult by overlooking this fundamental fact of life.

Elsewhere I have written about the wisdom of arranging a professionally supervised red-teaming of a request for funding. I'd like to reinforce that suggestion here. Success in arranging funding is mostly about getting ready and only to a lesser extent about making presentations. It is 80% preparation and 20% execution. The risks of being unprepared are substantial and often can prove lethal to a company's future.

The venture capital community is itself a tightly knit and interconnected group of professionals who regularly communicate with each other. They are dedicated to improving their results through professionalizing their decision-making process. The early stage investor community is a small part of the total venture capital community and even more tightly connected. Increasingly angel investor groups are behaving like the bigger venture fund managers. Their criteria for investment are tightening. Their expectations from founding teams are for more professional presentations as well as a more thorough going understanding of the company from the investor's perspective.

Navigating these dangerous waters without an experienced guide is like running through a darkened room full of furniture. Do yourself a favor. If you are going to start looking for early stage investment, get a guide – listen, learn and improve your chances for success. Give me a call or send an e-mail and I will be glad to organize a time to discuss how you can significantly improve your chances of being funded.

Presentations from the Investor's Perspective

All investors are bombarded with requests for meetings. Entrepreneurs put a lot of effort into networking and building relationships that will allow them to make a presentation to a possible source of funding. They have honed their elevator speech and given it many times. Mostly the results of these contacts are non-committal or an outright expression of no interest. All investors say no or maybe much more frequently than they say yes. But, there are the times when you say yes and a meeting is scheduled. Here are a few thoughts on how to handle that meeting.

Request an Advance Package: It is a very good idea to require an advance package; something considerably more extensive than the executive summary. This will allow you to go through the preliminary materials, request any additional materials or clarifications and do some diligence yourself. One of the ways to make this initial meeting more productive is to get very familiar with the details of what is going to be presented. This will also give you a chance to research the competition and prepare a series of questions or talking points. Providing some, or all, of these questions well prior to the meeting can go a long way towards making it more productive.

Set Expectations: Make sure that you let the entrepreneurs know how you would like the meeting to go. If it is scheduled for an hour, set the expectations for how that hour should be used. Their initial presentation should take up no more than half the time. This will give both you and them a change to discuss any issues or questions that come up. Setting expectations will also help them focus on providing the level of information that is appropriate. One of the faults of many presentations is that it is too detailed for an initial meeting. I have seen stacks of twenty five to thirty slides. You need to let them know what information you want to see presented. It is a good idea to contextualize the meeting in a broader process. Let them know what your procedures are following the initial presentation.

Avoid Redundancies: You have probably already heard the elevator speech and seen an executive summary. If the meeting is going to be productive, it should focus on new information. Some of these new requirements may not be covered in the package that they have put together. For instance, if you are particularly interested in their success developing paying clients or their advantages over the competition, a prior request will help make the meeting more productive. Make sure that you communicate your needs early in the planning process. You want to avoid simply going over materials that have been presented in prior, less formal conversations.

Outline an Extended Process: Many entrepreneurs get very excited when an initial meeting is agreed to. They approach it as if one clean stroke will result in their getting funded. Most investors I work with take between six and twelve months to make a final investment decision. The presenters should know that this is the first step on an extended journey. It is a good idea that, as a condition of taking the first meeting, your normal schedule is clearly understood. In some ways this will help the presenting team. Many entrepreneurs get very nervous that they will 'blow their chance'. You should make it clear that the initial meeting is only a prelude to an extended process. The likely outcome will be a decision to go the next step.

Watch the Team in Action: The initial meeting will be your first chance to see their team in action. Are they well prepared? Have they anticipated important questions? How do they deal with hard or unexpected questions? Do they understand your perspective? You can begin to assess the strengths and weaknesses which will determine the probability of their success or failure.

The first meeting should be a team presentation. It is a very good idea to open a file on each team member and keep notes on their performance. You will also be able to see holes in the team. Many entrepreneurs put together teams from the 'choir'. They avoid bringing skill sets onboard that are not directly focused on the technology. Often, when there are 'outsiders', they tend to be weak and unlikely able to meet their responsibilities. Three critical areas are business management, financial management and sales. Remember that you are assessing the team as well as their value proposition. One result of the meeting may be a set of recommendations for strengthening the team and an invitation to return once those recommendations are implemented.

Put them on the Spot: You need to know how the team and critical members will respond under pressure. They will certainly experience a lot during the period following funding. It is a very good idea to put them to the test very early in the game. Nobody comes to such meetings having all the answers to every question which will be raised. One of the things you should be looking for is the ability to say 'I don't know but will find out'. You need to weed out those who tend to try to bluff their way through such situations. Look for tensions within the team. Do they disagree without an apparent ability to resolve the disagreements? Teams that have figured out how to work productively together have a greater chance of succeeding.
Remember, it is one thing if the team is well

prepared for the presentation; it is another if they are prepared to build a business.

Highlight Your Needs and Expectations: Many teams will be used to presenting to the 'choir'. Your needs and perspective may be somewhat new to them. It is normal for entrepreneurs to see their company in terms of its technology and advantages over competition. But you will be looking at it as an investment. This need goes well beyond what might be presented in spreadsheets. Every seasoned investor knows that these projections are never accurate. Key members of their team need to understand that you are in it for the return on your investment. It the team does not understand how you are approaching investment in their company, problems are certain to occur with deviations from expectations. It is important to have a very clear understanding of those metrics that guide your decision and expectations.

Ask the Hard Questions Early On: Your decision process is probably going to center around a relatively short list of key questions. Some of them will be answered by simply being asked. Others will depend on your impressions. But, if you are going to stay on solid ground, you need to gather reliable and thoroughgoing answers to them all. A very good idea is to share most of them at the beginning of the meeting. "This is what we need to learn as a result of this meeting?" Be particularly sensitive to attempts by the presenting team to reduce the importance of any of these questions. Take that as a lack of seriousness and involvement in the process. Remember this meeting is fundamentally about you and meeting your concerns.

Avoid Answering Questions about Results: Your normal process will involve an extended subsequent discussion of findings, impressions and how well the investment opportunity fits your objectives. You may want to express an interest in continuing the discussion, but any expectation that you will be making an investment decision as a result of a first meeting is unwarranted and demonstrates a lack of understanding of the complexity of your decision making process.

Focus on Implementation: A key indicator will be the team's ability to implement. Look for relentlessness. They should be focused on monetizing the value propositions. One way to separate the 'science projects' from the nescient businesses is to look for clients or customers. Remember that old saying, 'amateurs have markets, pros have customers'. Unless you are investing purely in the intellectual property or the technology, the only way you are going to realize a return on your investment is through the creation of value in excess of your investment. The principal way that value is created is through building a growing and bankable client base.

An investment decision, particularly in early-stage companies, is a highly risky process. A structured and professional process will reduce lower the chances of negative outcomes.

Conversations with Investors – Chapter One

Jim Hunt of <u>The MITA Group</u>

In this series of chapters, I will describe several discussions that I had with investors in the Washington DC area. They range from angel investors to senior partners in well-established funds. I have known most of them for many years. That allowed us to cut through the usual PR crap and get to the heart of the process of reviewing investment opportunities. When I told them that my objective was to provide a series of chapters which would help companies seeking funding, each was very willing to help – it is, after all, in their interest to improve the process. I owe each of them a debt of thanks for agreeing to sit down and 'open the kimono' so to speak.

Visit with an Angel Investor

I have known Jim for many years. Like many angels in the area, he was a very successful entrepreneur. A seasoned veteran of the technology industry, over the past twenty years he founded and ran four successful technology companies. Jim founded and served as President and CEO of Ernst & Young Technologies, Inc., leading it to $75 million in profitable sales after just three years of operation. He then orchestrated the sale of EYT in late 2000 to Cap Gemini and served as President of the newly created Cap Gemini Technologies. Prior to his work at EYT and Cap Gemini, Jim ran a number of firms including BDS, Inc., a systems integrator focused on sales to the federal government. In addition to Jim's primary responsibilities as a line executive, he has helped launch and advise over a dozen companies in the high technology sector, with particular focus on software for federal and commercial markets. Much of his expertise has been directed at federal government market penetration for software application companies, system integrators, and IT service firms. In short, Jim has the experience to know what he is doing when considering an investment.

The Initial Screen

We sat down at a local watering hole and got caught up on the goings and comings of people and companies we knew. Then things turned to the 'interview'. I told Jim that I wanted to focus on how he decided whether or not to make an investment. My first question was, *"What percentage of the deals that come over the transom do you discard out of hand?"*

"Seventy percent of what I see is of no interest to me", was his reply. That means that only three in ten get any extended consideration at all. His principal reasons for discarding opportunities were 1) it's not in my area, 2) the team does not have the

necessary experience and 3) they don't have any adult supervision.

The first reason related to Jim's area of expertise – what he knew about and felt comfortable getting involved in. What disturbed him was the tendency of some founders to lump all funding sources into a single category. "*My history and investments are out there and easily found. People who don't take the time to see if their company matches my interests don't understand the process very well. I don't pay much attention to them.*" Jim's statement is certainly true for all the other investors I interviewed for this series of chapters. It is very easy to discover the interests and investment preferences of any established investor. People who do not take the time to match their company with those interests do themselves a great disservice.

Jim's second screen is another one that I encountered in all of my interviews. He avoids 'generalists' who seem to be the 'jack of all trades and master of none'. His focus is beyond the core technology of a company. "*It takes a wide range of skills to build a company. A limited number of them relate to the underlying technology.*" Jim looks for balance in the team. Do they have people who can handle the financial and HR needs of the company? These may be outsourced; but they need to be covered. Is there somebody who actually has successfully run a company – managed an extensive staff and budgets? "*If these are not present, I am unlikely to spend much time looking at the business plan*".

It was Jim's third screen that drew my attention. I had had experiences with the same syndrome – avoidance of adult supervision – and knew how important oversight was to the success of a new company. "*If a team balks at supervision, I don't spend much time reviewing their business plan*". The core truth is that everybody gets supervised in one way or the other. Recognition of that fact is a measure of maturity and evidence that the team understands how businesses are built. "*If the team seems to see the process as I give them money, they go and do what they think best with it and I get the results, I decline to play that game*".

"*How much time to you spend on each investment opportunity at this stage*", I asked?
"*I see about a deal a day normally. Most are discarded quickly. Of those that I have some interest in, I generally spend about an hour to an hour and a half deciding if I want to see the team and go further into their business plan*", was the reply.

The 30% Remaining

"*So, Jim, let's focus on the roughly 30% that make it through your initial screening.*

*What do you look for and what reasons
cause you to discard them?"*

Jim has four screens that he applies to
those that survive the initial culling. The first
is a more detailed review of the experience
and past successes of the team. He
focuses on the ability of the team to work
together. "*I want to see the tracks in the
snow – evidence that they have met and
mastered tough challenges in the past.*" For
Jim, resumes are not enough. He calls
upon his wide network to check on the
backgrounds and reputations of all the
people on the team. A weak link means a
weakness in the judgment of the founders.

Jim's second screen is a deeper push into
the question of 'supervision'. If he ends up
funding the team, he wants to know how
they will relate to him as an investor. Both
of us had encountered the hard-headed,
technocrat who has little use for people with
business backgrounds and experience.
We've also had our share of midget
Napoleons who seem to take a purely
instrumental approach to other people.
Good businesses are built through the
combined effort of lots of minds. Like most
investors, Jim avoids founders who tend to
push such help away and assert their own
omniscience.

If the teams pass the first two screens, Jim
then turns to whether it has a "*clear and
credible path to revenue*". His diligence in

this area extends far beyond the spreadsheets that come with the business plan. "*I check through my own network to verify their assumptions and reach out to their potential customers*". I am amazed at how few founders actually think that this might occur. Successful and well-established investors will always conduct such diligence. In many cases, the investor will quickly end up knowing a great deal more than the founders about the company's chances. How founders respond to this development is a very valuable character check.

All investors have their quirks and Jim's fourth screen evidences one of his. "*I look into the cash efficiency tendencies of the team. I don't invest with a founder who drives a leased car. I avoid teams with multiple family members on the payroll. If a cash-poor, start-up team has state-of-the-art electronics, I generally turn away.*" Jim has a aversion to investing in teams that seem to have a sense of entitlement – particularly if that leads to excessive spending on instant gratification toys.

10% of 30%

"*Jim, of the 30% that survive your initial screen, how many get all the way through and are seriously considered as investments,*" I asked?

"*About one in ten,*" was the reply. To put

that in perspective, over a ten-month period Jim might see three hundred deals. Of that three hundred, thirty might get a second and more intensive look. Out of that thirty, three might be seriously considered for investment. That alone should tell founders why the money chase so often yields null results. The odds of success with each investor are somewhere around three percent.

Time was getting on and we both had places to go but I could not help asking about the next stage. "*OK Jim, you have decided that maybe a team and their business plan may be worth an investment. What do you focus on next?*"

His first response was, "*I get to know the team better – watch them work together and see how they meet and overcome challenges – both with the business and in getting along.*" Jim believes that the team holds the key to the businesses' success. Their ability to work closely together sits at the center of their chances. He looks for indications of dissonance and conflict.

"*Sure, I do all the normal things like cleaning up the balance sheet, resolving existing personnel issues and aligning compensation plans. I drive deeper into the value proposition, investigate the intellectual property that the team controls, probe potential customers and work with the team to sharpen their business plan.*

But my investment is, first and foremost, in people. I am an early stage investor and people are the primary asset for such companies."

Conversations with Investors – Chapter Two

J. S. Gamble, Founder and CEO, Montis Group, LLC

In this series of chapters, I describe several discussions that I had with investors in the Washington DC area. They range from angel investors to senior partners in well-established funds. I have known most of them for many years. That allowed us to cut through the usual PR crap and get to the heart of the process of reviewing investment opportunities. When I told them that my objective was to provide a series of chapters which would help companies seeking funding, each was very willing to help – it is, after all, in their interest to improve the process. I owe each of them a debt of thanks for agreeing to sit down and 'open the kimono' so to speak.

The first chapter in the series focused on Jim Hunt of The MITA Group. Jim is a fairly typical angel investor – a successful entrepreneur who has turned to investing on early-stage companies. My next interview was with a close associate of Jim's whose background and experience makes for a different approach.

vive la différence

Every investor is different – they have different backgrounds and approaches to the process. This is one of the greatest lessons that founders need to learn. Each investor has a common characteristic – they have money to invest. But their life and business experiences are always more important than their bank balance. In the first of this series, I emphasized the need to match the investment opportunity to the interests of the investor. Many meetings are wasted because founders did not take the time to match their opportunity to the investor's interest. The lesson for this chapter is the need to match the presentation to the experience and tendencies of the investor – to realize that each investor is unique and will respond better if approached in terms they understand.

Visit with an experienced analyst

I have known JS for a number of years. He is Founder and CEO of Montis Group, which is focused on investing in and advising Early Stage Technology Companies. JS is an Advisory Partner of The MITA Group. In addition, he is a member of New Vantage Group, the Active Angel Investors of Vienna, Virginia, and a member of the Capital Access Network at the Dingman Center for Entrepreneurship at the University of Maryland. He is currently working with a dozen like-minded private investors to form a Group of Angel Investors focused on more active engagement with their portfolio Companies.

JS has a more academic bent when it comes to analyzing investment opportunities. He earned an MBA in finance at Wharton and is very experienced at building and testing financial models. As a result, he is murder on unprofessionally drawn business models and financial projections.

Currently JS is invested in or actively engaged with several early-stage Technology and Service Companies in the Mid-Atlantic Region. He served as Acting CEO of Smart Imaging Systems, Inc. and as an adviser to Agilyst, Inc., Semantic Labs and Wiser Together, Inc.

Prior to founding the Montis Group, JS was Senior Operating Executive in Broadband Cable and SVP of Wireless Operating Units with Comcast. He has more than 15 years of Full P&L (up to $1.2B in Annual Revenue) and CapEx responsibility. He had responsibility building teams focused on innovation, improving execution and launching new products and services to drive revenue growth.

Way back when, JS spent several years on the professional staff of McKinsey & Company, Inc. and Price Waterhouse where his clients were primarily telecommunications companies. He also served in various roles with GTE Mobilnet (Wireless Operations).

The Initial Screen

We met at Old Glory in Georgetown – a bourbon house that offers tables with a fine view of M Street. After chatting about deals that we were each involved in and people we knew, I turned to the interview. I told JS that I wanted to focus on how he decided whether or not to make an investment. My first question was, "*What percentage of the deals that come over the transom do you discard out of hand?*"

He knew that I had already done an interview with Jim Hunt; so the first response was a question. "*What did Jim say?*" I grinned and said, "*now, now – no cribbing. I'll tell you afterward.*" That was the first lesson from the interview. Angle investors in a given geographical region generally talk to each other frequently. They share information and track closely each other's success and failures.

"*Seventy-five percent of what I see is discarded out of hand,*" offered JS. (Jim's number was 70%). That means that, on average, three out of every four deals gets only a cursory consideration. His principal reasons for dismissing opportunities were 1) the business model does not hold up, 2) it's not in my area, 3) the founders are looking for a passive investor and 4) I don't know any of the principals or their advisers.

The first reason relates to how JS approaches the process of investing. Because of his background, he can take apart a business model and the attached projections quicker than most can review them. "*I look at their model and projections. I take them apart and test them against what I know. If I find obvious mistakes, I walk away quickly.*" His rule of thumb, "*I cut the projected revenue in half and double the time it takes to reach it and then I look at the results. My experience is that that is probably closer to the way things will turn out – that is, if they are successful.*" Other investors may get to the business model later in the process but JS goes there first. As a result, he may lose interest because your numbers don't add up or make sense.

His second screen it very similar to one that Jim Hunt uses. Good investors know what they know about and are very disciplined about staying away from investing in what they don't know. A particular type bothers JS. "*I see these teams who have reinvented themselves to fit the latest, newest, hottest thing.*" JS likes to see founders and management teams that are focused on what they know and have been successful with in the past. His investment is in the team's ability to execute their business model – not in the business model. "*Given a choice between a Superb Product/Model with Mediocre Execution and a Mediocre Product/Model with Superb Execution, I will take Superb Execution every time.*" This is an important distinction which ran through all my interviews.

The third screen is particularly important to JS. He likes to invest in situations that call for an active participation by the investors. This is a variation of Jim Hunt's third screen – 'they don't have any adult supervision'. JS prefers management teams that see a value in his or a co-investor's participation beyond providing the funding. "*I like situations that call for active participation.*" To be sure, there are investors who like to take a more passive role. It is counterproductive to approach an 'active participation' investor with such a proposal.

The fourth screen is one that many angel investors have and founders need to pay attention to. Many of these angel investors will not look at deals that do not involve one or more of their significant contacts. It is important to remember that angel investing is a much more intimate process than venture funding. Relationships and endorsements generally play a big part of any angel investor's decision to consider a deal.

"So, JS, let's focus on the roughly 25% that make it through your initial screening. What do you look for and what reasons cause you to discard them?"

"I look at the product or service that they plan to offer. My first question is does it

work? *You'd be surprised how many deals I see where the answer is negative or not yet. This investment round will get us there."* JS doesn't like to invest in science projects and isn't likely to fund product or service development. He expects the team to come with a fully developed value proposition. That's the case with most angel investors I know. There are those who will fund development; but a team needs to know ahead of time if the investor they are approaching is likely to make such an investment.

His second screen dealt with the path to revenue. *"I am fairly impatient with a team that has generated no customers. The proposition 'give us the money and we will generate revenue' does not impress me much"*, he offered. JS believes that good teams are compulsive implementers. *"The good teams are always selling – always working to generate revenues. The less impressive teams are always tweaking and fine-tuning their technology and avoiding the process of generating revenue as long as possible."*

JS likes to drill down deeper into the business plan and value propositions which underlie it. He sometimes finds himself pushing teams to consider details that they may have ignored. But his motive is far broader than testing the business model. *"I want to see how the team operates under pressure. I look for weak links – team members who are not up to playing their role. I drill down into the team, beginning with the CEO, and their capabilities as a team at the same time I am stress testing the business model and value proposition.*" He is likely to request one-on-one meetings with individual team members in order to come to an assessment of how their personalities and roles mesh. Gaps in the team are particularly serious negatives to JS that need to be recognized and resolved. He sees such team capability gaps and the plans to resolve them as a reflection on the judgment of the founders.

In his view the quality of the team is central to the chances of success. He explained. "*Most angel investors focus on the CEO – and the CEO is definitely important. However, I try to go beyond just the CEO to judge the larger Team skills, ID any gaps – for example, sales or business development – and try to judge how well the personalities/skills complement each other to make for a more effective Team. Some gaps are common and don't necessarily bother me. Companies can outgrow a Team member's capabilities; or, conversely, Cos. can grow into the skill 'sweet spot' of an experienced Team member. What can bother me is the CEO's recognition/non-recognition of the gaps and their clear or non-existent plans to resolve the gaps.*"

This approach allows JS to gather

information on a critical area – is the team willing to listen to alternative assessment, do they stay obsessively with their initial perspective or do they grow their understanding with detailed discussions and new viewpoints?

The 5% of the 25%

"OK JS, let's start with a hundred deals. You say that only twenty-five of them get any attention at all. What percentage of those gets a detailed analysis and now many are you likely to seriously consider for investment."

Every investor that I interviewed paused when asked this question. I suspect that was because the process has become so natural for them that they don't keep track of such things. Their interest is to find investment opportunities that are sufficient to satisfy their need to invest funds. That is a key to understanding how and why investors go through the process – often a frustrating one that can go on for long periods without surfacing a good investment opportunity. They have decided to invest part of their wealth in early-stage companies. Most founders do not grasp this dynamic sufficiently.

"I may take a closer look at about 20% of the ones that pass my initial screening", JS estimated. So, to run the numbers, out of every hundred deals that come to JS, he

discards seventy-five out of hand. Of the remaining twenty-five, roughly five get a more extended consideration.

"*And how do you go about making decisions about these few,*" I asked. "*I am working to satisfy my appetite for investment, balance my portfolio, manage the overall risk and make good investment decisions which will provide a hefty return,*" he replied. This response is important and every founder should work to understand what it means. Investors are working to balance a complex set of criteria, needs and objectives. Their decision is unlikely to be limited to whether or not they should invest in your company. In other words, you may be turned down for reasons that do not directly relate to your company.

We had enjoyed a couple of very nice bourbons and I a good cigar. Time and other obligations were tapping us both on the shoulder. But I could not resist one additional question. "*JS, I am getting the feeling that you see your role as extending substantially beyond that of an investor. Would it be fair to say that you see yourself more as a venture partner who happens to be providing funding?*"

"*I think that is more than fair. Sure I see the companies as investments. But I am a proactive investor and have confidence that I can bring much more than funding to the table. I am more likely to invest in a situation which calls for that involvement than in one which opposes it."*

Conversations with Investors – Chapter Three

Jack Biddle, Co-Founder and General partner, Novak Biddle Venture Partners

In this series of chapters, I describe interviews with investors in the Washington DC area. They range from angel investors to managing partners in well-established funds. I have known most of them for many years. That allowed us to cut through the usual PR crap and get to the heart of how they review investment opportunities. When I told them that my objective was to provide a series of chapters which would help companies seeking funding, each was very willing to help – it is, after all, in their interest to improve the process. I owe each of them a debt of thanks for agreeing to sit down and 'open the kimono' so to speak.

Interview with a Venture Capitalist

Prior to co-founding NBVP in 1996, Jack was President and CEO of InterCAP, a venture-backed computer software company. InterCAP was number 18 on the "Fast 50" list of the mid-Atlantic's fastest growing companies and was acquired by Intergraph in 1995. From 1987 to 1990, Jack rose from Senior Associate to Partner at Vanguard Atlantic, Ltd., a merchant banking group focused on M&A advisory work and control investments in software companies. At VAL, he served as turnaround CEO of a system software company and then as COO of an application software company. Earlier in his career he was an IT Industry Generalist, focused on Telecommunications Technology, at the Gartner Group, where he was also Executive Assistant to the CEO, Gideon Gartner. He began his career in 1983 in Austin, Texas at Business Development Partners, an early stage venture capital partnership. Jack holds a BA in Economics from the University of Virginia.

Jack currently serves on the Boards of WealthEngine, Vision Chain (Chairman), CorasWorks (Chairman), Triumfant, eMinor, ObjectVideo, Starfish Retention Solutions and Appian Corporation. Past Board or Observer seats include SafeView, Inc. (acquired by L3 Communications), Matrics (acquired by Symbol Technologies), Giga Information Group (Nasdaq: GIGX) (Lead Director), acquired by Forrester), Telogy Networks, (acquired by Texas Instruments), Tantivy (acquired by Interdigital), AnswerLogic (acquired by Primus Knowledge Systems), and Blackboard, Inc. (Nasdaq: BBBB). He is a Director of the Computer & Communications Industry Association, a member of Business Executives for National Security (BENS), and advises the U.S. Department of Defense on technology and innovation.

He is on the Investment Committee of the

University of Maryland's New Markets Growth Fund, an SBA leveraged fund targeting private equity investments in disadvantaged areas. Jack is a board member of TiE-DC. He is a frequent speaker on entrepreneurship for the U.S. Department of Commerce, and has made presentations for them in Russia, China and Japan. Jack is a Director and former Vice Chairman of the Board of the Baltimore Symphony Orchestra. He is a Trustee serving as Treasurer and Finance Committee Chair of the Sibley Memorial Hospital Foundation and also serves on the Hospital's Investment Committee.

Novak Biddle Venture Partners was established in 1997 to provide equity financing and assistance to the management of young, information technology companies. NBVP provides equity financing and assistance to the management of early-stage, information technology companies principally located in the Mid-Atlantic region. It is backed by a number of the country's most prestigious limited partners, and has over $580 million under management. They seek investment opportunities where the combination of ideas, dollars, experience, and relationships can create long-term, sustainable value. While they believe that the vast majority of business plans they receive have the makings of viable companies, they are looking for additional key features in the businesses in which they invest.

The Initial Screen

We met at the Novak Biddle offices in Bethesda. That was the first of many differences from the prior interviews. Jim and Jay run what are for all intents and purposes virtual operations. Like most angel investors, they keep overhead to a minimum. But Novak Biddle is a different kind of operation all together. They maintain a core staff of over a dozen professionals. NBVP prefers to be the first institutional capital brought into a business. Their target investment is from $100,000 to $10,000,000. While they focus mainly on information technology companies in the very early stage through first round, they will consider financing later stage opportunities and spin-outs where they can add significant value. They also will syndicate larger or later stage rounds through their limited partners and other firms in the venture community. Overhead is unavoidable consequence of their business model. With only two of us present, the Novak Biddle main conference room seemed positively palatial.

I opened the interview with my usual question. "*What percentage of the deals that come over the transom do you discard out of hand?*"

"*Ninety percent of the deals which come in are discarded out of hand.*" Those of you who have been following this series will recall that the two numbers for Jim and JS were 70% and 75% respectively. *"Why is the number so high"*, I asked. Jack responded with seven reasons:

- The company is outside of our geographical area of focus
- They are at the wrong stage
- They have not done any significant peer research
- We do not have expertise in their area
- Their business plan does not support a high-multiple exit
- The people on the team are not credible
- They are not working on 'hard problems'

The need for the first screen was particularly troubling to Jack. NBVP's website makes their geographical focus very clear. *"If you visit our website, it does not take long to see that we have such a focus. People who present deals that do not meet that focus have not done their homework."* This was a response similar to those put forth in the first two interviews. Investors provide a lot of public information on their interests. Teams which either ignore that information or, worse, never bother to understand it are generally dismissed out of hand.

The second screen is somewhat similar.

The statement at the top of the NBVP's home page is very precise. They provide equity financing and assistance to the management of early-stage, information technology companies principally located in the Mid-Atlantic region. Its mission is to help build successful, long-term, sustainable companies. The limiting word here is 'early-stage'. Jack paused and then said, "*We often do invest in pre revenue or seed stage deals. Blackboard was two guys with an idea and Lifeminders was one guy with an idea when we met. Probably half our portfolio was pre revenue when we invested. It's the ones that stay pre-revenue that we have a problem with.*" Founders who present start-up or pre-revenue companies will have a harder time getting Jack to pay attention. He has invested in pre-revenue companies in the past but, given the current state of the market, it is much harder now. Like many venture capitalists, it is revenue that really gets his attention.

Jack's third screen relates to the institutional knowledge of the Novak Biddle team. Over their years of investment experience, they have built up a deep understanding of the spaces which interest them. Teams which come in without a similar deep understanding are very likely to be turned away. "*We know our spaces very well. It's going to be a short discussion if it becomes clear that you don't know what you are talking about.*" This is an important lesson for founders. Most investors have accumulated a lot of information about the spaces that interest them. They spend a lot of time and effort keeping current. They expect that your knowledge will meet or exceed theirs. The best founders manage to exceed the investor's knowledge and bring them something new. I remember sitting in on one presentation during which a founder uttered the words *"we have no competition."* I don't think they even validated his parking ticket.

One of Jack's rules is that *"we invest in things we know a lot about"*. Over years of experience, most investors learn the importance of this rule. It's application is clearly evident in the listings of their portfolio companies. An idea has to be truly compelling if Novak Biddle is going to move very far outside of its areas of expertise. Founders who attempt to get them to stray from their strengths are generally in for a very short discussion. Remember, investors play to their strengths before considering the strengths of the management team or its value proposition.

The nature of the Partnership's business model dictates Jack's fifth screen. An old friend of mine was fond of observing that *"If you take a bear for a pet you need to be ready to feed it well – and bears do have an appetite."* Private equity and venture capital firms have a large bear to feed. They require a substantial and highly professional staff. Those people want to be paid well. The firms need to maintain substantial offices with all the attached overhead. As a result, only deals which have credible paths to high-multiple exits are going to attract their interest. And the key word here is 'credible'.

And speaking of credible, Jack puts a lot of emphasis on the credibility of the team. For him that means "*have they made money for me or others before*". If that sounds a bit mercenary, it is unavoidable. Novak Biddle puts its money on winners – winners with past successes which demonstrate that they are winners. Jack believes that the 'winner' pattern is set early in life. "*We like founders who have met major challenges – top collegiate athletes, successful business people and experienced team builders.*"

Jack's final initial screen focused on the nature of the problems that the founders were working to solve. "*We want to see a focus on developing solutions to hard problems. There is good business in solving the more pedestrian ones, but it doesn't often lead to the kind of high-multiple exits that we need to see.*"

"*That is quite a list, Jack,*" I observed, "*and it goes a long way to explain your high initial reject number. What you seem to be telling me is that the founders have to cover all these bases credibly before you are willing to give them a meeting.*"

"*That's right*", he responded.

The 10% Remaining

"*So Jack, let's focus on the roughly 10% that make it through your seven initial screens. What do you look for and what reasons cause you to discard them?*"

"*We look for an interesting, self-sustaining model. Then we ask 'can they get there'.*" Two critical components come together in this statement. Jack sees a lot of 'interesting models'. Most of them are not self-sustaining. Most often, after envisioning an initial push, the business plan becomes blurry and unfocused. Jack wants to see a vision that credibly extends well past the early stage. Sustainability is the key idea.

"*Then we look for high-margins preferably based on a proprietary advantage.*" High-margins are tied closely to Jack's fifth initial screen. The primary way to achieve a high-multiple exit is through a rapidly growing, sustainable business base with high-margins. A proprietary advantage gives a company a defensible market position. Both are necessary.

"*What turns you off at this stage,*" I asked. "*We avoid people who think of us as a bank*", he responded. Many founders unconsciously take this approach to investors. They treat investors as vendors of funding. Few stop to think of how insulting this is. Approaching a person like Jack, with all his experience, knowledge and connections – not to mention the combined resources of his organization – as a mere vendor of capital is to completely disregard the most important things that he and NBVP bring to the table.

"We look for founders who are 'coachable", Jack added. This echoed statements by the two other investors. *"We like to invest with over-achievers who have already demonstrated an ability to accomplish great things. These people are driven to be the best. I distinguish between those who say they are that way from those who have already proven to be that way."* Jack went on to describe eight characteristics of ideal founders.

- They have a history of success
- They are intellectually honest and not 'blowhard promoters'
- They are people magnets – teams seem to form around them
- They are coachable – seek out 'adult supervision'
- They are frugal – not prone to excessive expenditures or self-aggrandizement
- They have an extensive knowledge of their space
- They know clearly what they have to do to succeed
- They organize extraordinary experts

to solve hard problems

When I asked about the projections that normally accompany presentations, Jack responded that "*we pay more attention to the business model and the margins*".
"*So what part of the of the 10% get serious consideration*", I asked. "*Less than one in ten of those get a serious consideration?*" The less than 1%

"*Once we decide to take a serious look, we focus on the personalities of the major team members. We look for high-levels of personal integrity. Do they understand what we can bring to the table or do they think of us a bank? In the end, we are investing in people with ideas. Ideas are very common; very good people are far rarer.*"

"*You mentioned coachability, Jack. How do you look for that.*" I asked.

"*We get a real insight into coachability when we start to pounce on their business plan. These discussions are a real character test.*"

"*And how many of that 1% do you invest in Jack?*"

"*Maybe one in ten,*" was his response.

The State of the Industry

We had burned through more time than we planned, but I could not bring things to a close before I asked Jack about how the business had changed. He paused and then said, "*the venture business has become a lot less collegial. In the old days we all talked more openly. We knew each other and shared information. But now things are a lot tighter. Good quality deal flow is a lot harder to come by. High-multiple exits are a lot harder to achieve. I would guess that the business has not been profitable since 1997.*"

If you decide to enter the money chase, keep that in mind.

Death of the Hockey Stick

Here is a simple prescription for killing the tendency of founders to produce hockey-stick financial projections. Base the valuation of their company on the money being invested and let them 'earn in' to the extent they actually meet those projections.

~~~~~~~~~~~~~~~~~~~~

A recent phone conversation drifted into the question of valuation for start-up and early-stage companies. My own opinions on the matter have been formed through work with many such companies and on behalf of many investors in them. The 'traditional' approach to allocating equity between investors and management breaks down regularly – with both sides more than occasionally feeling that they are getting the short end of the stick. Some years back, I had the opportunity to try a completely different approach. The company had been taken through bankruptcy and 100% of the equity was held by the investors. Out of that situation, a new method of allocating equity emerged – one that seems to work very well even in the more normal situations of investors participating in start-ups and early-stage companies. Here is the thumbnail:

In my view, the correct valuation for early-stage funding is the sum of the investment plus a small amount for the founders. I then structure an earn-in program that allows the senior team to accumulate equity based on performance against pre-agreed to metrics. These programs can allow the team to achieve controlling interest in the company. I like this approach for two reasons. First, it virtually assures that projections are achievable in the eyes of management. The days of 'promoting' investors into a deal using hockey stick projections quickly fades away. Second, the plan allows investors to maintain a steadily increasing value while splitting the value created by the founders and management between the two interests.

The Money Chase - Should You

I attend a fair number of 'presentation events' over the course of a year. Mostly they have the same format. A panel of investors has been brought together. Applications for submission have been received from a wide range of start-up companies seeking funding. The applications have been reviewed and a lucky few have been invited to present. The room is packed with investors feeling important and the center of attention, nervous teams going over their last minute check lists and envious audience members. As the program advances, it is clear that many of the presenting teams have not asked a very simple question. Should they be in the Money Chase at all?

It is What We Do

I have put this question to dozens of teams and their responses have covered a wide range. But one type of response is particularly interesting. It goes something like this, "Of course we should be in the Money Chase. We are entrepreneurs and that is what entrepreneurs do." The first time I heard this, I was taken aback. I asked the team what they meant by it. It was clear from their replies that they had a particularly provincial and rather limited view of the process of starting and building a business. They obviously believed that the way you started a business was to get a 'good idea' and then find somebody to fund you. Having completed this process successfully, you were in business.

Although the understanding of this particular team was extreme, I have found that the general attitude infects many of the presenting teams. They see the process more or less the same:

- Get an idea
- Assemble a team
- Write a business plan
- Get an investor
- You are in business

When I tracked the origins of this understanding, I made a surprising discovery. Most of it originated during the time that one or more of the team had spent in a university entrepreneurism program. Some had degrees while others had attended seminars or belonged to programs that were affiliated with universities. The point is that their understanding of what it means to be an entrepreneur came intellectually before experientially. If you believe that starting a business is a journey from A to E, you are probably in for a rude shock.

The Costs of the Money Chase

Every hour you spend chasing investors is one you cannot spend chasing customers. At bottom, business is about having customers who pay you for your product or service. How much they pay you, when compared with how much it costs you to deliver, determines your gross margin. That margin is reduced by overhead. Overhead includes the time, effort and resources you commit to the Money Chase. For most start-ups, this cost is far higher than they realize. Here are a few examples:

The Distraction of the Senior Team: The overriding objectives of a start-up team should be to prefect and monetize the value proposition. Nothing else approaches that in importance. The Money Chase takes senior members of the team offline. Instead of pushing to meet these two objectives, they spend large chunks of time preparing and making presentations to investor groups. Such a talent drain may make sense after initial successes with customers, but it is seldom wise prior to that. Too many teams decide to chase money too early in the game.

A Dysfunctional Culture: The message that senior members of the team put out through their focus on investors can be very corrosive. "The real game is the money chase, not the business." If the Money Chase comes to dominate the activities of the founders too early in the process, the team will divide into two factions; the group that is chasing funding and the others who have been left at home to tend the fires. This is like sending your first-stringers out to the press conferences while having your back-up players actually play the game.

The Message to Potential Customers:
The role of the senior founders in building the trust that leads to potential customers becoming customers cannot be overstated. If a decision-maker is going to risk his job by going with a start-up, he will want to first build a strong relationship of trust with the CEO and other members of the senior team. What message does it communicate then the response is, "Bob is not available. He is busy with potential investors. You will have to deal with us." The answer is simple. It says to the potential customer, "You are not as important to this company as the Money Chase."

These are just a few of the costs. Chasing funding is a very expensive process. It can suck the energy out of a start-up and doom it to failure. In the very early stages, founders should be focused on the duel objectives of perfecting and then monetizing the value proposition. Until they can demonstrate an ability to do that, they should not be involved in seeking funding.

Threshold Conditions

So, what are the minimum conditions? How far along should a start-up be before it enters into the Money Chase? Here are a few suggestions:

Prove the Model: A strong team will quickly refine the value proposition and begin to generate revenues. These first steps are really the only way to prove that the company, and the team, has something that customers are willing to pay for. Most investors consider this a threshold condition for taking an investment opportunity seriously. If you cannot meet that minimum condition, you need to wonder why you are being allowed to present. The answer to that question may not please you at all.

Use of Proceeds: What are you going to use the money for? It may seem strange, but this question is most often very poorly answered by presenting teams. Good entrepreneurs get a lot of value out of each dollar they have to spend. Great entrepreneurs are parsimonious almost to a fault. But most of the presenting teams at these events have a sharply different vision. The largest amounts in their use of proceeds chart is typically for their own salaries. From an investor's perspective, this is very poorly spent cash. Sure, the team may take subsistence-level compensation until they generate sufficient revenues to cover their salaries, but they are getting equity in the deal and that should be enough. There are far better, much higher-impact, areas for using scarce financial resources. For a start-up to be investment grade, it should have already reached this point. Entering the Money Chase before reaching it is a waste of resources.

Wasted Overhead: Have you ever heard the saying, "He has more money than brains"? Well, start-ups can have more money that productive uses for it. The result is a waste of resources through spending that does not increase the chances of success. Even the anticipation of funding can exacerbate this tendency. I recently reviewed a business plan for a pre-revenue start-up. They were months away from having any customers, but the business plan and use of proceeds called for a fully developed team. They were planning to hire a Vice President of Marketing and a Director of Human Resources right away. They also had allocated funds for a senior-level Chief Financial Officer. The 'nut' for the full team overhead, before benefits, was going to be well over a half a million dollars annually. And this without dollar one of revenue in hand. Believe it or not, an investor funded the proposal. During my last visit to the company's well-appointed offices, I got the feeling that I was visiting a resort of some sort. Their corporate motto should be 'no worries'. But, of course, there is a worry. The cash will eventually run out, the investor will face a big loss and the company will go out of business. But for now, martinis all around! The hard truth is that flooding an early-stage company with funds too early in the process can seriously harm its chances of success.

A Few Good Rules

Deciding when to enter the Money Chase is one of the toughest decisions that any start-up team faces. Enter too early and you will siphon off time and energy in a hunt that has little chance of succeeding. Enter too late and your company will suffer from a lack of critical financial resources. Here are a few rules to consider:

Bootstrap as long as possible: Try to get as far as possible on your own resources. This is by far the least expensive way to build a business.

Be creative in tapping all sources: There are many sources of funding. Make sure that you do not overlook any of them. Many companies use government programs like SBIR and STTP to fill early-stage needs. Others pursue grants and similar sources. Some find potential customers that see their value proposition as good enough to support. Remember that venture funding will be one of the most expensive options. Also remember that it gets less expensive as your company grows.

Build the revenue: You have a much better chance of getting funding on favorable terms if you have customers. Remember the old saying, "Amateurs have markets and professionals have customers". The Money Chase gets easier if you are running a going concern.

Get your team working effectively: One of your principal goals in the early stages is to get your team working effectively. They should figure out how to generate customers and revenue. They should also learn how to respond to customer needs. Demonstrating this can significantly improve your chances and sweeten the deal you will eventually get.

Let your reputation attract investor interest: Remember that investors always have a hard time finding investment-grade opportunities. If you build an investment-grade company, they will seek you out. A good reputation for accomplishment will also open up alternate, less expensive sources of funding.

Hold off as long as possible: The further you get towards true profitability, the easier the Money Chase will be.

If you follow these rules, a strange thing may happen. The money will start chasing you. That is truly the way to win the Money Chase.

The Money Chase - Oil and Water

Very few entrepreneurs take the time to really study their company from the perspective of an investor. Those that do are often initially frustrated by what they see as a heartless and antiseptic assessment of the object of their passion and dedication. But, if they fight through those self-justifying tendencies and come to understand the investors perspective, they can substantially improve their chances of fathoming the process and, perhaps, of getting funded. The investor's world is quite different from the entrepreneurs in many ways. But there are also similarities.

Similarities

The most notable of these similarities is the fact that investors, much like entrepreneurs, make decisions in anticipation of a future which may or may not actually come to pass. Investors know that projections of future results are not the same as future results. They know that estimates are just that. The best investors use all their skill and judgment to make investments that will have a high probability of generating a very significant return. But, no matter how good they are, none can truly see the future.

Investors, like entrepreneurs, plant a flag every time they commit resources. They decide to put down a marker on this technology, with this team and on these terms. Once they have committed, they do everything within their power to help their investment pay off. In doing so, they are taking significant risks. They expect very significant profits in the form of a high return on investment (ROI). Like entrepreneurs, they are in it for the payoff.

Venture capitalists tend to be industry specific. Much like entrepreneurs, they focus on industries that they know. Many investors pick an industry focus because of personal experience, education or the anticipation that it will provide good opportunities for profit. Most entrepreneurs do the same.

Both investors and entrepreneurs are focused on building a reputation for success. Investors realize that their ability to raise subsequent funds will depend of the success of their current portfolio companies. The most successful venture capitalists have built a reputation for picking winners. As a result, they have raised a series of funds involving increasingly larger amounts of investment capital. Many entrepreneurs also look beyond their current company. They realize that a reputation for success will make it easier to fund a second or third company. These recidivist or serial entrepreneurs see their career over decades and as involving multiple companies.

Differences

The similarities pale in comparison to the differences. Bringing entrepreneurs and investors together is a lot like mixing oil and water. No matter how vigorously you shake the bottle, the mixture will, in time, separate out. But the fact that mixing these two perspectives is difficult does not mean that it should not be attempted or cannot be done. Both sides make efforts, some successful and others not, to understand where the other is coming from. Investors tend to see a lot more entrepreneurs than entrepreneurs see investors.

From my experience, the short-comings that often make the meeting of minds so difficult come from the founders. They simply do not put in the time and energy to understanding how investors think and what they consider a quality opportunity. The worst offenders are ones who rail against investors as stupid, lacking creativity, manipulative or arrogant. It is not just that this attitude, which you can track with a simple Google search, is insulting. For most investors, it reduces their interest in backing a venture involving such people and attitudes to zero.

My goal is to outline some of the differences between investors and entrepreneurs. My hope is that, by laying out some of these differences, I can help entrepreneurs better understand the vision and objectives of investors. Here are just a few of those differences:

Investors tend to spread their risks over a portfolio of companies. Even though they might group them within a particular industry, their approach to risk management leads them to invest a percentage of their funds in a number of companies. Unlike entrepreneurs, who have bet on a particular value proposition, in a defined market and with a specific team, investors diversify as a strategy. They protect themselves from losing all their funds because of one wrong decision by making a number of bets.

Here is how the average investor looks at the issue of risk management. Say they make ten investments over a period of two or three years. Their expectations are that at least two or three of them will prove very successful. The rest will fall into one of two categories. Either they will prove to be a total bust (and therefore written off) or limp along without managing the growth that was initially projected. The latter category is the most expensive for investors. They will need to become more involved in oversight and finding a way out of the investment. This approach to risk management is in sharp contrast to the entrepreneur who makes his bet on a specific technology, value proposition and team. Investors are more risk averse than founders.

When they look at a company, investors

see opportunities for putting capital to work. They are far less focused on the inter-personal issues that take up so much of a founder's time and energy. For investors, the company is primarily a set of spreadsheet projections, performance metrics and agreements which specify their rights and the returns they will receive under various possible outcomes. They will tend to tie the founder's interest in the company to their ability to meet the projections. This can be a real shock to founders who, prior to funding, consider that they own the company and are offering a piece of it to the investors in return for equity. Most professional investors consider a fair first-round, pre-revenue valuation as the sum of the funds provided plus a small margin for the founders. Performance metrics may allow the team to earn-in to a very large percentage ownership, but it is performance (successful and profitable implementation) that determines that ownership.

Most investors do not want to actively participate in the management of their portfolio companies. In fact, there are real liabilities if they act is such a way so as to be considered part of the management team. Their job is to make investments and monitor the results. This is true for angel investors as well as venture capitalists. The best investors have not been drawn from the ranks of successful CEOs or founders. In fact, these types have not historically done very well. They tend to be much more intrusive when it comes to managing the company and much less professional when it comes to evaluating investment opportunities. A friend of mine refers to them as the 'meddlers'.

Investors tend to have a much shorter time horizon. They are making the investment with the expectation of receiving a big payoff in the near to medium term. That means somewhere between two and five years. Their best results come through one or another type of liquidity event; a follow-on financing, sale, merger or public offering. In the best of all worlds, this event will 'cash them out' of the company. At minimum it will establish a higher valuation for their interest. Entrepreneurs are normally in it for the longer term. They maintain their interest in the company long after the initial investors have cashed out.

The core of an entrepreneur's world is a value proposition that is focused on delivering a product or service to customers at a price that will cover expenses and generate a healthy profit margin. The companies that they invest in are in the business of monetizing that value proposition. Investors have a value proposition as well. In it, the entrepreneurs are the customers. Their value proposition is focused on providing investment capital prudently and under terms and conditions which will generate acceptable levels of profit. Although this might seem like a similarity, it is one of the defining distinctions between investors and entrepreneurs. Investors have one client per investment. The founders and team are responsible for delivering the results which will give the investors a healthy ROI. The investors' focus is on making the investment under prudent terms and then insisting on the oversight and monitoring which will allow them to monitor progress towards the desired liquidity event. Companies have many clients. In fact, they need a growing customer base to be successful.

Investors, particularly venture capitalists, are normally managing funds supplied from a range of institutional investors. That means that they are managers of assets provided by investors who have decided to invest in their judgment and prudence. The source of their ability to make investments comes from others. Entrepreneurs are focused on creating value where none existed; using their own initiative, energy and skill.

Because investment funds are investing other people's money, they are bound by fiduciary obligations to carefully scrutinize potential investments. They are incentivized to pick winners. Given the rain of applications received, they tend to subject each to a superficial screen. That first pass is designed to eliminate the requests that suffer from superficial faults. Only requests which are well presented and include a credible business plan with a detailed revenue and expense projection, use of proceeds schedule, detailed analysis of competitors and comparison of value propositions are considered. Of these, only the ones that have already successfully monetized the value proposition are likely to be considered seriously.

Investors are constantly bombarded with requests for funding. As a result, they tend to be in a defensive or highly selective posture most of the time. Their review process amounts to whittling down a range of potential clients. Many are eager to receive financing but few will qualify and meet the investor's criteria. This process is generally time-extended. Investors are not normally in a hurry to make decisions. They prefer an orderly and extensive diligence process and negotiation. Entrepreneurs tend to want important issues resolved favorably so that they can move on to other things.

This brings me to the last difference I want to discuss in this chapter. Investors have standards which define an 'investment grade' opportunity. There are generally some very specific conditions which are essential before they will even consider committing funds. Here are just a few to consider:

The first of these is the demonstration that the team can successfully monetize the value proposition. To investors, that means delivering a product or service that clients have proved willing to pay for. Further, it means that the pricing structure leaves sufficient room to provide for overhead and a profit margin. Without this demonstration, most investors will not show much interest. They will gravitate towards those situations where the team has generated revenues and show that they understand the need to prove market acceptance.

Secondly, investors look to the composition of the team. They will be more favorable to a well-balanced, experienced team that has already demonstrated the ability to work together. Each team member will be scrutinized. Weak links will be taken as a sign that the CEO had poor judgment and weak team-building skills.

Thirdly, investors will look for assets that can serve as collateral in the event that the company is not successful. This may include founders' guarantees, personal assets, intellectual property and assignment of ownership rights. This protection is their insurance policy against catastrophic loss.

Finally, investors will look to the structure of the investment agreements and the performance metrics that guide the allocation of ownership. Their objective is to protect themselves offer a wide range of possible outcomes. If the company is very successful, they will be happy to own a relatively smaller percentage of the equity. If it barely manages to stay afloat, they will want to own most of it. In situations that require follow-on funding, they will most often require close to 100% ownership.

Oil and Water

Mixing investors and entrepreneurs is truly akin to mixing oil and water. But, the challenge is greater for the entrepreneur who wants the funding than for the investor who already had the funds. If you are going to successfully arrange the financial resources that your company needs, you have to understand how investors think and what they are looking for in an investment.

The Money Chase - Breaking the Truce

Venture funded companies exist in an uneasy truce between management and their investors. This is a healthy situation. The objectives of the investors are ordinarily different from those of the management team. Investors tend to see their participation in the company within the framework of an investment. They put up $X at the beginning of month one and expect to receive, at minimum, $Y within a fairly short time. For early-stage investors, a short time means anything from twenty-four to sixty months. They see themselves in a very risky business and attempt to mitigate that risk by spreading their investments over a portfolio of companies. Investors are in the business of extending their wealth.

The management team should be in it for a longer haul. They are interested in building the value of their equity; so their horizon might be ten or more years out. Entrepreneurs are in the business of creating wealth; theirs and members of their team. Their most likely exits are either retirement or departure under duress. Liquidity occurs when they are free to sell their interest in the company and there is a market for the shares.

If everything is going according to plan, this uneasy truce remains in place and everybody smiles at each other. But what happens when things start to go off the tracks?

The Ninety Percent

Roughly one in ten start-ups makes it to their fifth anniversary. The rest are what an investor friend calls 'road kill'. For one reason or another, they do not develop the traction necessary to take off. Sometimes they hit a wall and die quickly. This normally comes about when the team tries to monetize a value proposition that cannot meet market requirements. Some companies neglect to build monetization into their business plan and are still born. Other companies have a viable value proposition but lack the team to implement it. When the truce breaks down, there are several possible outcomes. Here, in order of declining catastrophic impact, are a few:

Signs

Forced Liquidation: This is by far the most extreme of the signs. Investors come to the conclusion that nothing will save the company; it is time to shut it down. Most of the time, investors will reach this conclusion during a series of private meetings and after extensive, and unproductive, sessions with management. Investors decide not to send good money after bad. Management is stripped of its prerogatives, told to pack up and leave and possibly will be subject to a series of lawsuits. The aftermath of a forced liquidation can get pretty ugly. There is lots of finger pointing and blame assignment. Investors will look for any way to recover their investment. Intellectual property will be the focus of a tug of war; which the investors almost always win. Assets will be sold off or merged into another company. Investors will want to put the memory of their investment behind them as quickly as possible. The entrepreneur and team will be branded as a failure and find it very hard to attract investors for a subsequent venture.

Invasion: Under this scenario, the investors move to take over the business. They have lost faith in CEO and team. This is a stark indictment of the management team. The investors have lost faith in the leadership's ability to monetize the value proposition. Further, they have lost faith in their ability to break out of the downward spiral. This is a major shift of roles for most investors. For the most part, they see themselves as money managers. They may be invested in half a dozen companies. Their vision of the process includes providing the funding, watching over their investment grow and then exiting with a profit. When an invasion takes place, all of that goes by the board. Founders will be crammed down or shown the door. Quite often the investors will have selected replacements. This process can move very quickly and takes some founders completely by surprise. Attorneys for investors will make sure that they have control of the intellectual property and other assets. Salaries will cease or be cut way back. If the team is allowed to remain at all, it will be with substantially reduced compensation and powers. Expenses will be carefully controlled and require outside approval. The company will be occupied.

Recapitalization: Generally referred to as a cram-down, a recapitalization means one thing above all; the interest that the management team has in the company is going to be substantially reduced, if not eliminated. A cram down generally occurs when a company has burned through provided funds and needs to ask the investors for additional investments. These requests generally carry the mark of failure. Investors are not generally pleased when a company fails to meet its performance metrics and turns to them for additional funding. The good rule is that every further chunk of inward investment is more expensive for the founders than the one before. Teams which fail multiple times to meet their performance metrics will find their interest in the company shrinking towards zero. Investors will, understandably, move to protect their interest in the face of such a systematic failure. The balance of power and the terms of the truce shift with each additional request for investment. Management can quickly find themselves little more than employees. A recapitalization is often a step towards selling or merging the company as investors work to at least recover their funds.

Changing the Team: In the beginning, investors fund a business because they believe that the management is capable and trustworthy. If they are professional investors, they establish well-defined performance metrics for the team and company. Failure to meet these performance metrics will undermine this trust. If the investors are less professional, they will have only vague performance metrics. But even these can go unmet. In both cases, evidence builds that the company is not going to be successful. The first tendency of investors is to look to the team. Sometimes they come to the conclusion that major surgery is necessary; as either an alternative or precursor to recapitalization. They may focus on individual members of the team or entire groups within management. The result is an intention to 'shake things up'. This response often occurs when a company has burned through the initial investment and is seeking follow-on commitments. Such requests give the investors pause and cause them to focus on the performance of management. Changes are in the wind. This often involves substantial changes in the management team. They will identify team members who are not pulling their weight. This could range from the CEO, who is not leading and motivating the team, through the CFO or controller, who is not maintaining adequate records. The rule of thumb is that, once this process begins, it usually results in the departure of a major chunk of the team. The greater the short-fall against expected performance is the more radical the changes that the investors are likely to insist on. The net effect is that the investors, not the CEO, will be calling the shots.

Changing the Value Proposition: If the team has been doing its job well but is not getting traction with customers, the investors may decide that the original vision of the founders was wrong. They will go back to the business plan and projections with the intent of finding where the company started to go off the tracks. This occurs when a core technology or service can be attractive to a range of customers. A company may have started with a focus on a particularly industry; only to find that potential customers do not have the ability to purchase it. Investors will drive management to reconsider that focus and shift to another group of potential customers. Once a new focus is agreed upon, there will be changes in the team; mostly driven by the needs of the new client base. Business development is one area that will feel the brunt of such a change. Marketing may be another. Shifts in value propositions almost always bring changes within the management team.

Increased Oversight: In most start-ups the

board of directors is relatively inactive. Initially, investors are not very interested overseeing the day-to-day operational of the company. They may take a seat on the board and will normally be satisfied to have a say in the strategic direction of the business. Oversight might include capital expenditures above certain dollar limits, decisions about expenditures for new product development, significant expansion of existing facilities or establishment of new ones, the sale of major assets, the formation of joint ventures, and management of the company's credit lines. Most management benefits by the discipline imposed by external oversight and from the experience of the board members. They can bring valuable experience and skills to the business and may sometimes even take on a semi-executive role, if so required. This arrangement provides the company with skills which it may otherwise not be able to afford." However, if the investors begin to worry about their investment, they will move to increase the oversight of the board. That is to say that, if the investors come to think that the company might be saved, they may reorganize the board. At this point the board becomes much more pro-active and invasive. Management will be asked to brief the board more frequently and in greater detail. Their decisions will be much more carefully and thoroughly reviewed.

The Shifting Balance

Entrepreneurs can go into denial when things start to go off the tracks. They look for reasons and think that having reasons is enough. This is a major mistake. Investors will not see it that way. For them, excuses are an unacceptable substitute for projected results. As the signs that the uneasy truce is starting to break down accumulate, management needs to conduct a clear and open gut check. The road that such a breakdown leads along is fairly well defined and none of the results are as favorable to them as getting the company back on track. It is up to the team to keep the investors in their 'money managers' role. The only reliable way to do that is to meet or exceed expectations. When the signs of stress start to appear, most of the options are in the hands of management. The longer these stresses remain and the more they increase, the greater the shift in prerogative to the investors. Unchecked, all of the cards will be held by the investors.

The Money Chase - Who They Do Not Invest In

The Money Chase is the graveyard of many a start-up. It can drain the energy and resources out of a new company and leave the founders frustrated and bitter. For many, seeking angel or venture capital investment is the most complex and subtle effort they have ever made. Most money chases fail because the founders do not have an investment quality company. The others fail because they either mismanaged the process or misunderstood how a successful money hunt should be managed. Yet others fail because they are simply not credible as entrepreneurs. This chapter is about that last group. Experienced angel investors and venture capitalist are always on the lookout for them and seldom take them seriously. Here are some types that they normally see and, for the most part, avoid:

The Crazy Eights

Man Have Got a Great Idea: The first group is the lazy and simple minded. Their clarion cry is, "*I have this great idea for a business and want to find somebody to make it into a going company. I am the 'idea man' but lousy at doing anything. So I am looking for a mule to pull my wagon and for somebody to give me five million dollars for the idea.*" Ideas are a dime a dozen and nine hundred and ninety-nine out of a thousand are pedestrian retreads of ideas that many others have had. Any angel investors or venture capitalist will tell you that they are constantly bombarded by these types. One of the reasons that they will not normally sign non-disclosure agreements is that they have seen almost every idea at least a dozen times and mostly from teams that have almost no chance of actually implementing and monetizing. If you are presenting to an investor who is experienced in your space, you should always start with the assumption that they have seen your idea before. Their questions will be, "*is this the team to implement?*"

Down the Rabbit Hole: Then there are the people who combine a Napoleonic complex with a rather loose grip on reality. These tend to be dismissive of the 'business world'. They regularly wrap themselves in the cloak of 'visionary'. (Beware of those who self-describe as visionaries as they almost certainly do not have the vision sufficient to see that they are not visionaries.) The details and 'little people' are of only minor interest to them. The world and the value of their company is self-manufactured and repeated over and over until it becomes a mantra. They have never subjected their product or service to potential customers for their consideration. Many will indicate that this is beneath them and the responsibility of the 'business types' that they will bring on board after funding. Whatever wonderland they may inhabit, I can assure you that it is of no interest to investors. They are interested in making a sound investment that will yield a big return; period, paragraph. Let the Mad Hatter and the March Hare enjoy their tea in private.

It Is Just Me and the Mice: I call this type the 'Lone Ranger'. One of the essential skills that a founder needs to have is the ability to draw together a well-balanced team that can refine and monetize a value proposition. If they cannot get A-level people to join their team and put shoulder to wheel during the early stages, their leadership, value proposition and ability to actually build a company comes sharply into question. You have to have a good team that can prove that there is a significant market for your product or service. Venture capitalist and angel investors may take meetings with Lone Rangers but they generally are just doing research into an area that interests them and seldom will consider seriously making an investment. One may have a good idea but it takes a team to build a profitable company.

I Had Some Spare Time: I call these the casual entrepreneurs. Their approach to starting a business is passionless and often very clinical. Successful entrepreneurs are a blend of dedicated, focused passion for their value proposition and hard-headed, parsimonious persistence. They are easy to spot because both of these characteristics are consistent over time. Good entrepreneurs are also always restless; searching for ways to increase their chances of success. They are constantly asking about their competition, the strength of their value proposition and how to improve their team. Casual entrepreneurs present a stark contrast to this. They are diffident about their company, slovenly in their attention to details, less than interested in the competition and confident that their chosen level of engagement and energy will be sufficient to win the day. The key work here is sufficient. It almost never is.

A Gambler with Your Money: There are a range of these types but they all have one common characteristic; entrepreneurship is a gamble to them. When I was at the Sloan School, MIT I took several courses in entrepreneurship. Afterward I helped manage in a number of studies focused on defining an entrepreneur. We had a very good pool of successful founders to work with and that helped establish a baseline for the research. One finding stood out above all; entrepreneurs really successful entrepreneurs are risk averse and active and aggressive risk mitigaters. An example might help. We asked our entrepreneurs and a range of wannabe entrepreneurs to take a series of tests. Some of them were games. One was a ring toss game. The game was simple. Each person was given a set of rings and a peg to toss them towards. Every time they got the ring on the peg, they got points. If they missed they got no points. But, as this was the test, the farther back from the peg you stood the more points you got if the toss was successful. The pattern that emerged was fascinating. The wannabes divided into two groups. The ones who openly defined themselves as entrepreneurs went to the far wall and 'shot for the moon'. Their logic was that, even though they have a minimal chance of scoring, when they did the score would be big. The group that thought they might become entrepreneurs someday took a different approach. They stayed very close to the peg and often dropped it on; making sure that they scored the maximum number of successful tosses. Our real entrepreneurs took a very different approach. They gradually backed up until their skill was good enough to hit the peg most of the time. They worked to maximize the total points earned by balancing the risk of failure against the chances of success. In other words, they were neither gamblers nor accountants; they were entrepreneurs. Investors are very diligent in avoiding the gamblers and accountants; entrepreneurs are who they invest with.

Implementation is for the Proletariat: Business is generally ten percent about the idea and ninety percent about monetization of that idea. Many founders have this attitude and I have heard more than one state it in front of investors. My comment is always, "*if implementation is all about the proletariat, then the investor should find some proletariat and invest in them*". The 'implementation test' for the founders begins when they first pull a team together. It continues as they face the challenge of building a paying customer base. No founder is truly an entrepreneur until he demonstrates an ability to get others to pay for his product or service. Prior to that he is just a student with a class project. Investors are always on the lookout to avoid these types. They come in a wide range. Some are the perennial founders. They have an idea that they have been pursuing for years. Some might have well developed prototypes and well-worn business plans. Others may not have gotten as far as the prototypes stage and have only a business plan and a set of crude drawings. Still others have nothing but the idea and maybe a website. The common characteristic is that they cannot seem to significantly monetize their value proposition. One of two reasons seems to drive this. The first is that they see implementation as beneath them. The second is that they do not have the energy and dedication to do it. Either way, investors will not be interested.

Do Not Know, Do Not Care: I am always amazed by the number of founders who get a meeting with a funding source only to demonstrate that their knowledge of the competition is far less developed than that of the investor. I call these the blasé crowd. Any experienced investor will automatically begin doing diligence on the competition of proposals that they agree to consider. Many of them have researchers who specialize in doing exactly that. The good ones never agree to a meeting until the file is fully packed with information about both the competition and potentially disruptive technologies. In short, they know a great deal about the competitive landscape before the first meeting occurs. They do this for two reasons. The first is to satisfy themselves that the value proposition is well based and not vulnerable to being trumped by either existing or potential competition. The second is to be able to test the presenting team's knowledge in these key areas. If it becomes clear that they know more about the competition and disruptive threats than the team, the meeting usually comes to a quick and firm ending. Lack of key knowledge in critical areas is considered sufficient reason to end consideration of the investment.

I am Learning All the Time: Sure, your ability to learn and learn quickly is important to investors but they are much more interested in what you know and how that can be turned into a going business. There is a group of entrepreneurs who seem to think that failure, and the associated waste of resources, is justified by the lesions that they have learned. The core of this fantasy is a lack of direct connection to the ruin that failure brings to the wide range of people involved. Many of these were surfaced in the aftermath of the bubble bursting in the late 90's. They, for the most part, walked away with firmly packed bank accounts while their employees and investors were left to deal with the loss.

There are many more 'types' that investors routinely avoid. Angel investors and venture capitalists sit through a lot of presentations in the course of a year and see almost every kind of founder that they want to avoid. It is never a tragedy when one of the crazy eights is identified and avoided. But it is a tragedy when a legitimate proposal from a competent team is dismissed because they carelessly tagged themselves as one. And it is a tragedy when a team fails to avoid becoming one of the crazy eights.

The Money Chase - One Way to Avoid Being Avoided

There are many 'types' that investors routinely avoid. Angel investors and venture capitalists sit through a lot of presentations in the course of a year and see almost every kind of founder that they want to avoid. Of course, there is a complication. Sometimes the presenters unwittingly give the impression that they fall into one or another of these categories. It is never a tragedy when one of the bad apples is identified and avoided. But it is a tragedy when a legitimate proposal from a competent team is dismissed because they carelessly tagged themselves as one. Investors have to make lots of decisions in relatively short order. It is important not to give the wrong impression in these early meetings. A bit of creative preparation goes a long way towards avoiding such an outcome.

One of the best ways to assure that you are taken seriously is to red-team your presentation. This is a proven method for improving the chances of success. It is not rocket science nor is it very difficult. It is a straightforward and logical approach to a recurring challenge. If you are out to win, read-teaming has to be one of the tools in your toolbox. The process is designed to make sure 1) that the proposal correctly addresses concerns of the investors; 2) that the information offered would meet their needs; 3) that key questions are answered and superfluous ones avoided; and 4) that the team presents and defends in a highly professional, well informed and effective manner.

A red team review is arguably the most important step in the entire cycle of preparing for and delivering a presentation to potential investors. This approach which will improve chances for getting funded. The core of the process is a group of people who will evaluate your request for funding, and your company, from the investor's perspective.
Red team members read your materials as if they were evaluating it for funding. This means that they will not be advocates for your company. Quite the opposite; if your presentation has serious problems or if they don't get what you're trying to say, it will more likely be, "*This is not making sense as an investment!*"

That in itself is more than a lot of VCs will do. They are in the business of finding opportunities and making investments; not critiquing your presentation. Many times all you will get is "*Thanks for coming in – we will get back to you if we are interested.*" But a red team goes the extra step; its purpose is to help you improve your chances of getting funded. In that role they play hardball; team members can be very critical, step on your toes if necessary, and pull no punches. A red team member who holds back honest and incisive criticism because of a fear of hurting someone's feelings is not helping the effort.

Red teaming can be a very unsettling experience for some founders but the goal of each and every member of the team is to help improve the presentation, value proposition, business plan and chances of getting funded. Remember, to make a success you occasionally have to break a few egos!

Here are some guidelines to follow for forming and running a red team review:

- Because of their experience, members of our red teams need to be able to emulate the process and mindset of the VCs that the company is going to present to.
- You should pick at least three people to serve on the team.
- They need to be knowledgeable in the company's space.
- Team members must have no prior connection with the company that is presenting.
- They must be willing and able to commit the necessary time and attention to the process.
- You should insist that members are given at least two days to read the materials to be used in the presentation and do a bit of personal research.

- Team members must be committed to helping you improve their chances of getting funded.

Benefits of a Red Team Review

This independent review procedure emulates the investor community's initial-review decision making. It simulates first meetings with VCs and critically reviews the presentations. The process also delivers an in-depth, interactive debriefing of a funding request. The results will provide you with guidance and direction on what must be done to improve your probability of being funded.

Red team members read and research materials and discuss them among themselves prior to your actual presentation.

The team then sits through your presentation as a simulated initial meeting with a potential investor. The focus of the evaluation is on how well you presented your business plan, value proposition and answered the threshold questions that an investor is likely to ask.

Finally, the team delivers a thoroughly interactive debriefing. The focus is on specific recommendations for resolution of major issues. They also present recommendations and guidance on improvements relative to strengths, weaknesses, opportunities and threats.

The Money Chase - What Does Investment Grade Mean - Part 1

Entrepreneurs frequently enter the money chase much too early in the game. They often start as soon as they have a business plan finished; if not before. Most presentations that investors see fall into this category. The results are beneficial to the investors because they get regular insights into developments within a space they find interesting. But the story is far different for founders. They end up making presentation after presentation without any progress towards funding. For many start-ups, this series becomes a death spiral. Founders end up spending more and more of their time chasing then having meetings which result in little but a polite "don't call us, we'll call you". They get increasingly desperate as reserves dwindle and finally disappear. Finally run out of money, options and energy. Exhausted emotionally and financially, they frequently decide that it is time to 'get a real job'.

The hard truth is that this is an appropriate fate for most start-ups. Somewhere around one in ten makes it to their fifth anniversary. Many never generate significant revenues; some none at all. Angel investors are keenly aware of these statistics. Most have developed screens to keep from investing in losers. They want to identify that very small percentage of early-stage companies that have the value proposition, team and business plan which will put them in the top ten percent. The best investors identify likely losers very early in the process. This keeps them from spending time listening to presentations that will not result in an investment.

I have frequently used the term 'investment grade' to describe the type of investments that attract the attention of investors. I want to outline some of the characteristics that can put a company in this category. But before I start, a cautionary note is prudent. Investors come in all sizes and shapes. Their individual characteristics and objectives drive them in directions that are impossible to sum up within the span of a short chapter. The following list is not a panacea as, indeed, no such a thing exists. But, it may help entrepreneurs focus their efforts in ways that make it more likely that their money chase will end with funding.

Implementation

Investment grade describes a proposal that merits careful consideration because the entrepreneurs seem to have a very good chance of turning their company into a profitable and scalable business. It is important to realize that simply saying that that is your intent is insufficient. Too many 'entrepreneurs' do that. Most investors are averse to these kinds of 'after you give us the money, we will do as we say' proposals. True entrepreneurs are masters of implementation and of the creativity that is required to do great things with very limited resources. Investors look for signs that the entrepreneur and team are reflexive implementers. Here are a few signs they value:

Customers: Investors expect that they will be providing funds for a business focused primarily on generating revenues. The first thing that they look for is evidence that the value proposition is being monetized in ways that will generate revenues. Here, the old saw applies, "amateurs have markets: professionals have customers". If you make a presentation to investors without any indication that you have successfully market-tested that value proposition in the 'real world', your position will be significantly weakened.

Movement Forward: The team is on trial from the very beginning. That trial gets more exacting the moment the business plan is finalized. Investors expect to see progress on implementing the plan. They see too many proposals that seem to have been still born; where the team has worked the business plan and then come to a full stop until funding has been arranged. Agility and Adaptability: No plan gets implemented as originally written. The mark of a good entrepreneur is the ability to change focus and approach on the run; as circumstances merit. However, this coin has two sides. Investors are leery of founders who either change their plan at a whim or refuse to change until it is too late. Agility and adaptability are seasonings in the recipe. Too much means that the entrepreneur is not sufficiently dedicated to the core value proposition. Too little means that necessary adaptations will not occur.

Perseverance and Determination: Good entrepreneurs are truly a force of nature. They move through obstacles or move them out of the way. A well balanced and focused entrepreneurial team has the same characteristic. The best are determined to win the battle with the weapons and resources at hand. This characteristic is hard wired. By that I mean that truly entrepreneurial teams will start implementing from the very beginning. They will constantly amaze investors with what they can accomplish with limited resources. Remember, investors are trying to decide if this particular company is 'investment grade'. They are much more likely to come to that conclusion if the team has wrought miracles with limited resources. Plants that flourish in resource-poor soils are likely to thrive when fertilizer is added.

Initiative: Investors are always avoiding entrepreneurs who cede the initiative to events beyond their control. They avoid teams what come to a dead stop because a funding decision has not been made, a key piece of technology has not been developed or the business plan has not been finalized. One investor had a particularly interesting way of focusing this issue. He added up the total number of hours that a team had at its disposal during a given week and then compared it with what they had accomplished. The results were sometimes startling. In one particular case, he came to the conclusion that the founders had to be spending most of their time playing video games as they got so very little out of the hours at their disposal. Another entrepreneur made a presentation with a business plan that had a two year old date stamp on it. He was asked, "in the two years since this plan was completed, what have you accomplished"? The silence that followed brought the meeting to a rapid conclusion. Every presenter needs to be aware that they are being graded primarily on the results they have already achieved. Having a business plan and an untested value proposition is not nearly enough. Being an entrepreneur is about implementing. Without that, you are just an author of third-rate fiction.

The Money Chase - What Does Investment Grade Mean - Part 2

In the first part of this series, I outlined the general characteristics of an 'investment grade' opportunity. I also described how the process can so easily end up being a waste of time for both investors and entrepreneurs.

Entrepreneurs frequently enter the money chase much too early in the game. They often start as soon as they have a business plan finished; if not before. Most presentations that investors see fall into this category. The results are beneficial to the investors because they get regular insights into developments within a space they find interesting. But the story is far different for founders. They end up making presentation after presentation without any progress towards funding. For many start-ups, this series becomes a death spiral. Founders end up spending more and more of their time chasing then having meetings which result in little but a polite "don't call us, we'll call you". They get increasingly desperate as reserves dwindle and finally disappear. Finally run out of money, options and energy. Exhausted emotionally and financially, they frequently decide that it is time to 'get a real job'.

I then discussed the very first focus of most investors; the implementation of the business plan. Investors are very leery of teams that write plans and then come to a full stop; hinging future actions on some event such as funding. Next I would like to discuss what it usually the second focus of most investor's diligence efforts.

The Value Proposition

Most investors will next focus on the value proposition. Here 'investment grade' involves questions of scalability and sustainable margins. This is how business generates revenues and profits. In general terms it goes something like this; we will offer X at a price of Y to a defined customer base. X is important because it solves the following problems that those customers face. The value of the solution we provide exceeds Y. We have demonstrated that this is the case by already developing a list of paying clients. It costs us Z to offer the service. The difference (Y-Z) is our gross margin. Investors want to see such a formulation demonstrated by the team. Fictionalized descriptions of how good it is going to be post-funding are not going to impress them much.

Established Markets and Customer Bases: The fascination with cutting and bleeding edge technologies that so dominated the buildup to the bubble bursting in the late 90's is a thing of the past. Investors know that early adopters generally do not fair very well in the long term. They prefer investment opportunities that involve established markets and well established customer bases.

Thoroughgoing Knowledge of the Competition: One of the common failures of entrepreneurs is that they do not develop a thoroughgoing understanding of their competition. With the advent of search engines like Google and Yahoo, it is very easy to establish a working knowledge of the competition. Most investors reflexively conduct such searches. The tragedy is that so many entrepreneurs do not. During many a presentation, it quickly became evident that the investors knew much more about the competition than the founders. They had two advantages. First, because of their interest and experience in the space, they regularly saw similar presentations. Second, they did the searches and analyzed the competition. An entrepreneur who presents in such an environment is almost certain to be shown the door; after the investors have added to their own knowledge of the space.

Competitive Edges: Knowledge of the competition is only a first step. Once gathered, the information needs to be used to define the extent and durability of any competitive edge that a company might have. Successful entrepreneurs are very good at this process. The know how to dispassionately view their value proposition from the perspective of a potential customer. In the end, that is the telling challenge to any value proposition; will the customer choose it over the competing ones? The best way to accomplish such an analysis is to subject it to a SWOT analysis (strengths, weaknesses, threats and opportunities). A professionally drawn business plan will focus heavily on such an analysis. It will also document the systematic testing that went into validating the value proposition. Founders who have not done this will be considered not to understand the competitive environment that their company intends to operate in.

Disruptive Technologies: One way to point out the potential costs of disruptive technologies is to generate a list of products and services which were at one time the basis of an industry but have now been overtaken by alternatives. For example, the vinyl LP was superseded by the eight track tape; only to be replaced by the cassette. The cassette fell to the compact disk which is now giving way to electronically transmitted music and information. The fax and copy machines are also examples of technologies that are giving way to a convergence of technologies. And how many remember the rolodex? Investors are looking for value propositions which will maintain competitive edges well beyond their participation in the company. Discovery of a potentially disruptive technology will be enough to turn them away; particularly if the entrepreneurs are not aware of it.

Customer Validation: The most potent validation of any value proposition is customer acceptance. Most experienced investors will not substitute their judgment for the customers'. Until customer acceptance is a proven fact, presenter will be asking investors to do exactly that. Founders need to realize that such a request is likely to be declined. Investors who find a value proposition attractive may simply wait until they see a presentation by a team that has obtained customer validation. In the meantime they have received a free education on developments within the space.

Margins and Overhead: Investors are very sensitive to how value propositions that might be commoditized. Commoditization means shrinking margins. Too many investors have had the experience of providing funds for a company that assumed their margins will either stay the same or increase only to find that commoditization has sharply reduced them. It is not sufficient to demonstrate that early margins will be substantial. If a company is going to thrive, it needs a value propositions which maintains margins and allows for controlled overhead. If, for example, a company will have to make substantial investment in ongoing research and development in order to remain competitive, investors will assess the team and its potential to stay ahead of the game.

Technological advantages are very hard to maintain and easily lost. When lost, margins either shrink or disappear.

As you will no doubt gather from the above, the issues surrounding the value proposition are much more complex than a simple analysis of the product or service being offered against the possible pricing structure. Investors are very sensitive to the ability of the team to monetize any value proposition. The more progress a team has made in that direction, the better its chances of being funded.

The Money Chase - What Does Investment Grade Mean - Part 3

In the first chapter in this series I offered a general definition of 'investment grade' and discussed the first issue that most investors look at. They generally start by asking are the entrepreneurs implementers or discussers? Most investors have had bad experiences with founders who are 'all hat and no cattle'. The second screen that most investors use is a close evaluation of the value proposition that the company is based on. They are interested in sustainable margins and scalability. Investors want to see that the value proposition has been market tested and has resulted in a growing list of referencable customers. This helps the investors answer a series of fundamental questions such as:

- Is the company in a space that interests us?
- Are the founders dedicated to implementing the business plan?
- Do they understand the space they are working in?
- Do they have customers or markets?
- How adaptable and agile have they been?
- How determined to succeed are they – before they get our money?
- How compelling is their value proposition?
- How well do they understand their

competition?

- What are the tracks in the snow and how do they augur for either success or failure?

Once those two screens have been passed, wise investors turn to evaluating the team that the founders have assembled. Strangely enough, this is one of the areas where founders fall down rather badly. Many teams are cobbled together out of the people who happen to be in the room. Sometimes these people receive inordinate amounts of equity in the company and they are almost always given titles that are far above their capabilities. Good investors are likely to analyze any team in a more exacting fashion than it has ever been assessed before.

The Team

Investors are looking for 'investment grade' teams and pay close attention to each member of the team. They work hard to identify these teams and will go an extra mile or two with them. Many entrepreneurs slap together a team out of people that are conveniently available. Often they focus on the part of the team that is closest to their own area of interest and experience. The other functions are 'casually covered' by amateur add-ons. They then often try to cover the weakness with high-sounding titles; Chief Financial Officers who are really controllers, Vice Presidents of Human

Resources who are really recruiters. Investors generally sense if this is the case and avoid serious discussions. Their aversion is easy to understand. Entrepreneurs who take this approach are more likely to be gamblers who take the easy way around unfamiliar challenges. A highly professional team is the mark of founders who have taken a serious approach to seeking out and bringing on board A-level talent. It is important to remember that the team is one of the first assessments that any investor makes.

Resourcefulness: This is such a key part of any successful start-up that it is hard to understand why so many founders do not focus on it. Resourcefulness means getting every advantage out of the resources at hand and exceeding expectations through that effort. It involves a focused and disciplined use of the sweat equity that is so central to any new company. It also means creatively tapping into pools of resources, financial and human, that can move the company forward.

Uniform Strength: Investors look for 'holes in the team'. They are particularly sensitive to a lack of business experience. One of their nightmares is investing in a research project that never even begins to monetize the value proposition. Early indications that this might be the case are often discovered by reviewing the background and experience of team members who are not directly associated with the underlying technology. Sometimes these functions are not covered. One presentation by a group of programmers comes to mind. The team was completely made up of programmers. When asked about the business model or projections, they responded dismissively. The investors responded in kind. A well balanced team will have high quality members who bring experience in the business of business. Any company is, after all, first and foremost a business.

Experience: Investors have a number of types that they are always on the lookout for. One is the serial failure entrepreneur. If a founder has had a series of failed attempts to start a business, investors are not likely to provide funding for the latest. They take it as a weakness that the prior attempts have resulted in lost resources and funding. A second type is the 'entrepreneur' who thinks that going into business is a way to get rich. This may sound counter-intuitive but it is, in fact, a good indicator of impending failure. Investors want to provide funding for founders who have a passion for the value proposition that their company stands for. For the most part, entrepreneurs do not get rich; at least not quickly. A third type that investors avoid is the 'I was a consultant for years and now have decided to get into business' person. Good investors take a long, hard look at the resumes of key team members. For them, the past is prologue.

Successful entrepreneurial activities will give them some confidence that the founder and team have a good chance to build a profitable business.

Skin in the Game: When investors evaluate the team, they put heavy weight on evidence that they have real skin in the game. That means more than their time and future prospects. Investors frequently hear the following, 'we are committed to this company and will dedicate our careers to making it a success'. Of course, the fine print reveals that they expect to draw a salary and have their expenses covered. Investors see such proposal as really being, 'hire me as a consultant with equity, and I will work as long as you pay me'. The root of failure for most funded start-ups is that investors have settled for exactly that; companies run by well-paid consultants. Teams that can demonstrate that they have significant skin in the game and are willing to have scarce financial resources used for other purposes than paying their salaries are prized by investors.

Focus on Winning: There is a difference between winning and talking about winning. All entrepreneurs do the latter; most of them do it very well. Investors immediately set about sorting out the talkers from the doers. Talkers tend to become paid consultants and poor investments. Most experienced investors have had the experience of providing funds in the hope that talkers will turn into doers; in other words, they have lost money. So, how do investors identify the doers? They look for tracks in the snow. Doers are always doing and that is the difference.

Board of Directors: Investors take the presence of a casually formed or non-existent board of directors as a sure sign that the founders are not willing to subject themselves to effective oversight. Most investors avoid entrepreneurs who see themselves as cowboys or 'lone rangers'; in other words, ungovernable. They also avoid the self-righteous, self-certifying types who either cannot or will not learn and grow. A well-structured and operating board provides a range of important services in addition to their fiduciary responsibility for protecting and extending shareholder value. Three of these are succession planning, compensation alignment and audit review. It is a mistake to assume that, simply because a company is early-stage, these services are not important. It may take a creative approach to involve outside directors; but oversight is essential to success. There is one formulation that investors are particularly averse to; the CEO who also wants to be Chairman. The combination of these roles is normally a bad idea, but, when the CEO is a relatively inexperienced entrepreneur, it can be a recipe for disaster.

Board of Advisers: There are two kinds of

advisory boards. One is focused on the technology of the company and serves as a strategic adviser to senior management and the board of directors. The second is focused on generating revenue and is populated with high-profile and well-connected individuals who can reach and influence decision makers. Most investors see the first type as evidence that the founders do not have the depth and breadth of knowledge necessary to run their company. Some have seen trade secrets and competitive advantages leak out through such boards. It is the second type that really attracts investors' attention. An advisory board made up of four to six very well connected, committed and experienced people, who are committed to pro-actively representing the company to key decision makers, is seen as an asset and indication that the founders know how to put together an aggressive business development team.

It is rare that investors will come to the conclusion that the team is exactly right; that it needs no 'tweaking'. They will often suggest additions to or replacements for the team. Most investors also realize that a team needs to evolve over time; that the people who help get the company off the ground will probably not be the ones that take it to its first ten million dollar year. Teams are, by their very nature, dynamic organizations. Investors do well to make sure that the CEO understands this and can manage the very difficult balance between

loyalty to those who have rendered service
and loyalty to the needs of a growing
company.

The Money Chase - What Does Investment Grade Mean - Part 4

In the first three parts of this series of chapters I discussed major areas of focus for investors considering funding a company. Briefly, they were:

- Implementation – Are the founders implementing or just talking about implementing once they get the funding?

The Value Proposition – How scalable is the business model, what are the margins and are they sustainable? Have the founders proven that they can monetize the value proposition?

The Team – Is the team balanced, experienced and operating as a team? Are there weak members? Are they a team or a gaggle? What are the tracks in the snow that show that they can build and manage a company?

Generally these and many more questions have to be answered satisfactorily before a professional investor turns to the financial projections provided by the founders. Amateurs will start with them, but this is more an indication that they are amateurs than anything else. Financial projections need to be analyzed within the context of well developed and tested knowledge of the team that is providing them. Otherwise, you are looking at a series of spreadsheets that may or may not be realistic or reliable projections of an achievable future.

Projections

One of the two most dangerous pieces of software is Excel (the other is PowerPoint). They support a shallowness of analysis and a facility with manufactured fantasies that result in presentations that seem sensible on the surface but have no direct relationship with reality. 'Investment grade' projections are well based in direct experience and connected directly to the monetization of the value proposition. When reviewing a presentation, investors pay attention to these issues to a greater extent than to the actual numbers on the spreadsheet. Consequently, the projections that come with requests for funding tell investors a lot about the founders and their team. Most investors pay a lot more attention to the structure and attention that has gone into producing them than the actual numbers themselves.

The Hockey Stick: There is something about this fiction that almost every entrepreneur feels a need to salute. It is a central part almost every business plan. Year one revenues are zero, year two a bit better and then, in year three, the hockey stick starts to kick in. To be fair, investors have done as much to perpetuate this fiction as entrepreneurs. It is almost considered required by both sides. Entrepreneurs are trying to establish a valuation that will cost them as little as possible for the funding. A valuation of a million dollars will yield a forty percent equity exchange for four hundred thousand. One of four million dollars will reduce that share to ten percent. But, of course, the valuations are completely fictional. There is a better way. The correct valuation for early-stage funding is the sum of the investment plus a small amount for the founders. Such an approach shuts down the con game. The founders are compensated according to their ability to deliver. Such an arrangement will contain an earn-in program that allows the senior team to accumulate equity based on performance against pre-agreed to metrics. These programs can allow the team to achieve controlling interest in the company. This approach has several advantages. First, it virtually assures that projections are achievable in the eyes of management. The days of 'promoting' investors into a deal using hockey stick projections quickly fades away. Second, the plan allows investors to maintain a steadily increasing value while splitting the value created by the founders and management between the two interests. Third, it establishes clear performance metrics from the very beginning; before any investment has been made. Fourth, such a plan will only be attractive to teams confident of their ability to deliver; paid consultants will wilt under the bright light. Finally, this approach melds the perspectives of both sides into a solid, working framework.

Use of Funds: Investors generally divide the use of proceeds schedule into two broad categories. The first includes expenditures which are directly connected with the development of a going business while the second lists overhead and related expenses. The latter category includes the salaries and benefits paid, expenditures for equipment and supplies not directly related to delivery on the value proposition and other 'perks' that the team includes. Most investors are very leery of presentations that show a very high percentage allocated to this second category. One extreme example was a 'Use of Proceeds' schedule that provided for full salary payments to a fully expanded team from day one. In this case the company was pre-revenue and not expected to generate revenue for the first full year. The investors regarded this team as 'paid consultants' and quickly came to the conclusion that the company could not afford them. Another example was a schedule that provided for purchase of sophisticated laptops and cell phones for the entire senior team. When asked why this expenditure was necessary, the response was 'we need to establish a successful image'. The investor, to his credit, patiently explained that such an image was established by successfully generating revenue; then showed them the door. Good entrepreneurs understand that scarce financial resources should be used in ways that generate customers and revenues. Overhead is corrosive of that objective. Investors know this and look for teams that act on this wisdom.

Validation of Revenue Projections: A while back there was an advertising campaign that ended with the line 'if you can do it, it's not bragging'. The validation of a revenue stream is not a complicated process. You offer; they buy. You invoice; they pay. What they pay exceeds the loaded cost of delivery. You have a margin. Margins are good if they are positive. Investors regularly sit through presentations that attempt, by an amazing variety of ways, to avoid testing, let alone validating, the value proposition. Some entrepreneurs go on and on about how huge the market is, how much it is projected to grow and how even a small percentage of that market will make them all rich. This is all a smoke screen and most experienced investors know it. The smoke is designed to hide a serious flaw in the business plan; the value proposition has yet to be validated. One presentation comes to mind. A team was presenting to a front-line venture fund. They offered projections of first year revenues that were impressive. What they forgot was that the starting date of those projections was six months past. The senior partner asked a simple question. "You are half way through your first year; what is your revenue to date?" The meeting was over.

Parsimonious but Adequate Expenses: That is how many investors describe their preferences. They comb through the expense projections and connect each item with the process of generating revenue or advancing the value proposition. They know that the best entrepreneurs are very good a squeezing a lot of value out of each dollar. They also know that, if they are going to realize a return on their investment, every dollar has to be well spent in generating that return.

Provisions for Forward Investment: This is one of the most contentious issues. The balance between monetizing the value in hand and increasing that value is individual to each company and situation. Too much forward investment will drain funding away from the process of generating current revenue. Without that revenue, there is no company; only a class project. Too little forward investment will reduce the rate of added functionality and increased value. The true arbiters in this situation are the customers. They will tell the team what value they are finding and how that value can be improved. That is why it is essential to generate customers early on. Any discussion of forward investment that does not involve paying customers will likely be without a solid foundation.

Projections are either an honest and

outright attempt to communicate likely outcomes or a cynical and manipulative attempt to induce an investor into an arrangement designed to disproportionately favor the founders. Most experienced and sophisticated investors have the ability to make the distinction and avoid the latter. Most entrepreneurs do themselves a disservice by attempting such a swindle for two reasons. Firstly, they will lose credibility with the more professional investors; the ones who could probably help them the most. Secondly, they will quickly and negatively brand themselves and their company. The investment community is fairly tight knit and bad experiences get around faster than good ones.

The Money Chase - What Does Investment Grade Mean - Part 5

In this installment of the series I want to focus on exit strategies. The first and most important thing to realize is that the expectations and, indeed, objectives of investors are necessarily different from those of the management team. The investor's time horizon extends, by definition, only so far as a liquidity event that will allow them to recover their capital and realize a substantial profit from having taken the risk of investment. The management team needs to take a much longer view. They should be interested in building the company, and their wealth, far beyond that point.

One red flag is when the founders seem to have the same expectations as they do. This sometimes happens when investors fund companies headed by one of their 'stale CEOs'. Many funds maintain close relationships with founders that they know and trust. Often, and sometime in concert with one of these CEOs, they will come up with an idea for a company. In these situations, the CEO tends to have the same exit expectations as the investors. The result is that there is no truly long-term vision for the company. Its culture becomes purely instrumental and self-serving. Personal greed, rather than effectively servicing the needs of the customers, dominates that culture.

Exit Strategies

Every definition of 'investment grade' must include a description of possible exits by the investor. It is important to realize that it is the investors' definition of 'exit' that is the issue when talking to them. Although investors may pay token attention to management's long-term prospects, they have a far different set of expectations when it comes to exit strategies.

Investor Perspective: The investor perspective is driven by their approach to providing funding. They are approaching their participation in the company as an investment. This is a critical point. Investors are not treating the company as an investment; they are focused on their ownership in the company. Their analysis and expectations are driven by a calculation that begins with the investment and ends with its repayment with profit. Once their investment and profit have been recovered, the company will be a fading and hopefully fond memory. They will seek other opportunities for investing their funds. Investors are generally invested for short and medium periods. They always want to see the back door or doors as they enter the front.

Entrepreneurs Perspective:
Entrepreneurs, on the other hand, need to see their company as a long-term

commitment; an investment of their time, resources and energy. Investors will respond negatively if the founders clearly intend to exit at the same time as they do. They are looking for a team that is making a long-term commitment to the company and value proposition. Good entrepreneurs value the welfare of their company over their own welfare. Founders who adopt the investors' approach to exit strategies are not going to meet that standard.

Future Funding Needs: Most investors know that they will probably not be providing all of the funding that a company will need during its growth. They will structure their agreements to take into consideration the possibility of follow-on funding. They will also pay particular attention to the fate of earlier investors. One extreme variation of this second consideration is called the cram down. If investors are providing second or third round money, they will want to see most of their funds used to grow the company. They will also want to get as large an interest in the company as possible. Earlier-stage investors will want to see part of that new funding go to paying them back for their investment. Teams need to realize that this tension is unavoidable and to work with all parties to reach an agreement that will receive broad support and advance the interests of the company.

Downside Exits: Few people go into

business to fail. But the hard fact is that only one in ten companies makes it to their fifth anniversary. That means that in nine out of ten times investors have to face the challenges of a downside exit. In business, as in life, breaking up is hard to do. Most of the time the investment agreement will guide the process. In the absence of such an agreement, things can get both chaotic and very messy. It is in the interest of all parties to have worked out the details of what will happen if the company fails to get the traction necessary to flourish.

One of the hardest things for entrepreneurs to understand is that investors do not see their company through the same lenses as they do. The best entrepreneurs are following their passion and building a business that they can be proud of. It is off-putting to have someone view it purely as an opportunity to make money. Many entrepreneurs recoil at this vision and cannot bring themselves to respect investors for who and what they are; the providers of the very funding that their company needs in order to grow towards their vision of it. the formulation is simple: Investors provide funding as an investment. Their expectations are to recover those funds along with as big a profit as possible and in as short a time as possible.

The Money Chase - What Does Investment Grade Mean - Part 6

The objective of this series has been to describe the characteristics of a company that make it attractive to investors. The series began with the realization that many entrepreneurs sometimes do not have the ability to see their company through the eyes of the people they are hoping will fund it. The result of this disconnect is often tragic and seldom edifying. Companies that should be funded are not. Businesses that should have a chance to get off the ground and onto a path to profitability do not get that chance.

It is important to start with a single fact. Most start-up companies do not even approach being 'investment grade'. Most entrepreneurs have never been investors in companies. They do not have the experience or knowledge that would allow them to understand the dynamics and risks of the process. Most are so fixed on getting funded that they do not take the time to assess their company from any perspective but that of its financial needs. This can lead entrepreneurs to a one-dimensional view of investors and the process of approaching them. Nowhere is this misunderstanding more evident than during the preparation for and presentation to potential investors.

Entrepreneurs tend to know little about the people they are presenting to; even though there is often much information available given a slight effort to collect it. They tend to see the process as one of 'selling' the investors on the opportunity to help build a company and lead with the technology and competitive advantage that they suppose they have. But, as you have read in the first five parts of this series, investors do not look at things that way. They find little value in a presentation that appears to be designed to recruit them as team members. In fact, they are frequently irritated by the pretension and misunderstanding of the situation that drives such a wild pitch.

The Presentation

Presentations give investors an early insight into the quality and professionalism of the entrepreneur and team. Remember, most of them see dozens of presentations within the space of a given year. Because they focus in particular spaces, they may end up seeing the same or similar slides, hand-out materials, analysis and statistics again and again. Whole sections of business plans may be repetitively inserted by local consultants who specialize in writing business plans. If the plan and presentation appear too slick and pre-packaged, investors will tune out quickly. If it is filled with special effects or broadly crafted 'visionary' statements, they will also turn away. Investors prefer to hear about companies and teams that are already in business, implementing, establishing and defending margins, building an expanding customer base, subjected to effective board oversight, with an effective financial control and reporting system and looking for funding to expand. Most of them prefer to fund expansion rather than R&D. The most effective presentations begin with a list of invoices sent and evidence of payments received. Here are a few guidelines:

Concise and to the Point: It is a shame to have gone through all the trials of producing an investment grade company and then loose the opportunity to get funded as a result of an inadequate presentation. Yet some entrepreneurs do exactly that. There are a number of reasons why this occurs. The most common is that they focus their presentation on issues that seem important to them; rather than the ones which are important to the investor. This happens when the founders make the mistake of thinking that they are presenting to someone who is as involved as they are in the underlying value proposition and is interested in the 'neat' advances that the team has come up with. Although this may be of some interest to investors, they are principally focusing on the company as a potential investment. In other words, they are much more concerned with progress of implementing the business plan, in monetizing that value proposition, in the generation of strong and sustainable revenue streams, the control of expenses, the likelihood that the company will achieve strong acceptance with a growing customer base and, finally, the path to a successful exit. Another mistake that many entrepreneurs make is to misunderstand the appropriately limited agenda and goals of each meeting. They come to an initial meeting loaded for bear. Their slide stack might total twenty or more and be very complex with lots of dense graphics. They pass out printed materials that go into the details of their 'competitive edge'. Then they drone on and on. The investors come to an initial meeting with a short list of questions. If the presenters are not smart enough to realize that, the reception they get will not be positive. It is important to understand what questions the investors will be focusing on and to deliver clear and convincing responses to them.

In Their Space: It is important to remember that, if you are presenting to the right investors, they will have seen lots of presentations and many of them may be close variation on yours. By far the best way to get funded is to seek out investors who have made a commitment to your space. They will have spent time sitting through similar presentations. Many of these investors will have a broad understanding of the space, competition and challenges that the company will face in getting traction and customer acceptance. Entrepreneurs who present to such investors with the attitude that they are unsophisticated and inexperienced are likely to get a rude shock. The best first presentations involve less than ten slides and, along with collateral materials, focus on the issues that concern the investors during the initial meeting.

In Your Own Words: Investors are very leery of pre-packaged presentations and business plans. They can generally recognize one that has been written by a consultant. Remember, they have sat through many such presentations. If they see close variations of the same slides that were presented to them last week, they are certain to assume that either the same consultant put together the materials or the team cribbed from another business plan. Investors want to receive a presentation in your own words as a demonstration of how well you understand your space, value proposition and challenges. They will assume that, lacking your willingness or ability to do just that, you are either lazy or amateurish. Neither one will give them confidence.

Realistic: When investors are sitting through a presentation in their space, they being a wealth of historical experience to the table. That means that they have seen similar presentations from other teams. The value propositions and strategy for monetizing it have been discussed; sometimes many times and in great depth. Market assumptions have been challenged and tested. Discussions of differentiating advantages have been proposed and tested. Teams have been challenged with inconvenient facts and have had to respond. In short, you are presenting to some very well educated and knowledgeable people. Based on this experience, they have a pretty good idea of what is possible. They generally can recognize a poorly grounded fantasy very quickly. They may have 'test questions' that are designed to gauge the strength and depth of knowledge that the team. A single misstep can bring the presentation to an abrupt end. Many entrepreneurs make the mistake of overselling. Experienced investors know how difficult it is to build an expanding customer base at price points that yield good margins. They are also familiar with the sales cycle in your space. A presentation based on overly optimistic margins and shorter than normal sales cycles will be greeted with skepticism. Remember that your judgment and prudence is on trial; not just your entrepreneurial zeal.

Performance Metrics: Investors are particularly attracted to presentations that involve sharply defined performance metrics; particularly ones that control the compensation and ownership of the team. The more thoroughgoing the metrics the better. It is not sufficient that they focus on meeting revenue projections. Metrics should extend to the performance of all aspects of operations; including overhead, equity ownership, compensation, board of directors structure and responsibilities, advisory board operation and performance, research and development and marketing. The last four are notoriously left out of most performance metrics schemes. Metrics should form the core of the funding agreement. They should be detailed enough to anticipate most probable outcomes and provide pre-defined resolutions to the most likely disagreements.

Most entrepreneurs see presentations to investors are seminal events. That is a mistake. Such presentations should be a review of the seminal events that have preceded them. By that I mean that a proper way to begin is to focus on past successes; particularly when they involve winning customers, collecting revenues and establishing margins. Investors know that the future, particularly for start-up companies, is hard to anticipate. The past, however, is known and knowable. Most are willing to consider the past as prologue; as an indicator of a likely future. A presenting team without such seminal events is at a major disadvantage. It is, after all, far easier to describe what you have already accomplished than to spin a credible tale about what you may accomplish in some uncertain future.

The Money Chase - What Does Investment Grade Mean - Part 7

When I first started this series of chapters I had no idea that it would extend to seven. I also did not anticipate the level of interest in the topic. Many who read the opening chapter had not thought of the question 'how does my company stack up against a professional definition of investment grade'. Others had thought about it but not in any systematic fashion. It is always gratifying to write about something that readers care deeply about. It is even more gratifying to engage them in discussions that result from that writing.

Once you grasp the ideas behind 'investment grade' the question logically occurs; "how can I improve the investment grade of my company?" Of course, there are no short answers to such a question.

Making the Grade

The foregoing chapters do not presume to provide an exhaustive list of metrics but they should give you some idea of the standards that you have to meet in order to be considered 'investment grade'. There is little that you can do to polish the apple if your company does not meet these requirements. You need to keep moving forward until it does. Entering the money chase before you have an investment grade company can be a kamikaze raid on a vacant lot. The effort will take up lots of your time; find you giving away any competitive edges and ending up with nothing to show for the campaign. It is a hard thing to analyze your company in a dispassionate cold, bright light. You have to force yourself to do exactly that. Here are some suggestions that will help you along.

Red-Teaming: When you prepare a presentation for funding you run the considerable risk of becoming so close to the trees that you grow less and less capable of assessing the forest. A professional, independent review of your funding request, well before you present it to the first investor, could make the difference between being funded or wasting a lot of time; yours and the investor's. The best way (in fact, the only reliable way) to make sure your presentation is well focused and provides what an investor requires is to have it reviewed by an objective panel that sees it through the eyes of a potential investor. A red-team looks at the presentation exactly that way. They evaluate the request for funding, projected use of proceeds, business plan, value proposition and management team as if they are being asked to invest in the company; looking for weaknesses and strengths and checking to make sure threshold questions are addressed in a way which will lead to the next level of discussions. The composition of the red-team is critical. Avoid industry insiders. Pick people who have been in the investor role. The responsibility of the team is to test your company against the standards of 'investment grade'. Have an independent adviser, who is experienced in red-teaming proposals, organize the team. The first time you see the red-team should be on the day of the presentation; just like it will be when you actually present to potential investors.

Patience and Prudence: This chapter began with an observation that most entrepreneurs start the money chase much too early and it is appropriate that we revisit that issue towards its end. Timing is everything in business. Too early and you are not ready to meet the challenges; too late and you are past your prime. But the money chase is one of those races where maturity and demonstrated capability trump youth and energy; or as the old country song goes, 'old age and treachery always overcomes youth and skill'. Entrepreneurs should learn what it means to be investment grade. They should learn it from the perspective of the investor; not from their own as the CEO of a company in need of funding. It is not the need that should drive the money chase; it is the effort to become investment grade. That means that patience and prudence are essential to the process. A founder should have the patience to develop the company so that it qualifies for serious consideration by investors. They should be prudent in reigning in the tendencies to try to get funded as a way to solve all their problems. Most of the challenges of early-stage businesses are not solved through funding; in fact, funding can make many of them far worse. The challenge of getting every value possible out of each dollar is best learned in a climate of scarcity. Developing a team that can work together effectively is best done when there is pressure on the team to be creative under pressure. These are components of a solid foundation and should be well in place before the superstructure is build with investor dollars.

If You Build it They will Come: By far the best situation that a company can find itself in is being chased by investors. Remember the old saying, 'bankers only want to lend you money when you don't need it.' The variation here is that, 'you are in a stronger position with potential investors if you can walk away from a deal that gets too expensive'. Investors hate to say no, but find it stimulating when a company they have approached declines to take their money. The further along you can bring your company before you seek investment, the better your chances of getting funded on very favorable terms. Here is another way of looking at it; the more clearly your company is 'investment grade' the easier it will be to get it funded.

Red-Teaming - Improve Your Chances of Getting Funded

This is a proven method for improving the chances of success. Not rocket science – nothing very difficult – just a straightforward and logical approach to a recurring challenge. If you are out to win – this has to be one of the tools in your toolbox.

~~~~~~~~~~~~~~~~~~~~

The beginnings of a good idea

Recently I sat in on a presentation that two founders of a technology start-up made to a front-line venture capitalist. What was most striking about the experience was that, from one point of view, the founders seemed very well prepared. Their presentation was polished and contained all the usual sections, their slide show was professional quality, and they spoke with passion and deep knowledge about their space. The materials which they provided were all neatly and professionally packaged.

But early in the meeting it became apparent that the team was not prepared for what they were encountering. Their pitch was clearly more appropriate for a group of fellow technologists. They had not taken into consideration the predictable concerns and perspective of the person to whom they were presenting. The VC had interrupted the flow of their pitch with a couple of completely normal threshold questions and it went downhill from there.

After the session I asked the investor how frequently this kind of thing happens. He shook his head and responded "More often than I would like and far more often than needs be. The tragedy is that it doesn't have to." When I asked what he meant he replied "I'm probably the first outsider that they have ever given this presentation to. As a result their pitch comes to me without any real critical review. But what is most discouraging is that their entire presentation was not focused on my concerns as an investor but on a 'preaching to the choir' gathering of their peers. And what they don't seem to realize is that mine is a very tight community and we talk to each other on a regular basis. What these guys did today was not only establish a negative brand with me but with any others that I end up talking to about them."

I immediately understood what he meant. One of the services I provide to clients is the establishment of an advisory board designed as a high level, business development engine. I had built such a board for a company that is in the enterprise level software business. One of the company's proudest achievements was that they had earned a high level of certification for their software development process. This certification was prominently mentioned in all of their promotional materials and on their website.

The senior management team was presenting during the first ever gathering of the board. The advisory board consisted of five very high-level individuals with an average of three to four decades of experience. Most had built businesses or run very large organizations. All of them had risen to the top of their profession. This first meeting was designed to bring the board members up to speed.

The software certification was prominently displayed on one of the earliest slides that the chief operating officer presented. One of the board members interrupted the pitch with a question, "OK, I'm one of your customers. Other than making your software more expensive, what is the value of this certification to me?" It quickly became clear that any answer which the team could offer was focused on the 'choir' – those individuals who had already bought in to the value of the certification process. They were not able to provide an answer from a client's perspective. As a result, they lost the confidence of the board and had to work hard to get it back.

As I related the story my friend nodded and ruefully smiled. "I'm glad to see that this happens to other people. I had taken to thinking that mine was the only profession that encountered this kind of thing."

As we talked and told war stories, a

conversation with a former partner in the movie business came back to mind. Sy had been talking about how much more difficult it was for new talent to get experience since the demise of a vast network of performance venues that used to serve as incubators. Again, there was the pattern. People need a space where they can knock off the rough edges and focus their presentation.

What came out of this was a vision for a kind of 'presentation boot camp' – a space where founders could refine and focus their pitch without incurring the liability of having to learn under fire – and avoid establishing a negative branding in front of potential investors to boot.

Borrowing from another space

I first came across the idea of red-teaming years and years ago when I was working in the government contracting space. I subsequently learned that it is also widely used in the commercial sector. A proposal team will subject the results of its efforts to a panel of outside experts well prior to submission to the client. The process is designed to make sure 1) that the proposal correctly addresses the RFP; 2) that the solutions offered are ones that would likely be accepted by the client; 3) that the costing of the proposal has been done correctly and does not contain any extraneous expenditures and 4) that the team can present and defend the proposal in a highly professional and effective manner.

This process is standard procedure – in fact, widely considered an essential part of best practices – in the government contracting space. The danger of not following these best practices is severe. I know companies which, in the re-bidding process, failed to adequately challenge the proposal team and lost contracts that they should have won.

When you prepare a presentation for funding you run the considerable risk of becoming so close to the trees that you grow less and less capable of assessing the forest. A professional, independent review of your funding request, well before you present it to the first VC, could make the difference between being funded or wasting a lot of time – yours and the VC's. With our knowledge of the investor's decision making process and wide range of contacts within the VC and private equity communities, I can organize and facilitate a red team review that can significantly improve your chances of being funded.

Red teaming can be applied with considerable benefit to testing and refining presentations to venture capitalists. This process can assure that it meets the needs; adequately address is the concerns; is clearly and professionally delivered and definitively answers the threshold questions that the investor is likely to have.

Red Teaming a Request for Funding – the Right Way

The best way (in fact, the only reliable way) to make sure your presentation is well focused and provides what a VC requires is to have it reviewed by an objective panel that sees it through the eyes of a potential investor. A red team looks at the presentation exactly that way. They evaluate the request for funding, projected use of proceeds, business plan, value proposition and management team as if they are being asked to invest in the company; looking for weaknesses and strengths and checking to make sure threshold questions are addressed in a way which will lead to the next level of discussions.

A red team review is arguably the most important step in the entire cycle of preparing for and delivering a presentation to potential investors. I have developed an approach which will improve chances for getting funded. The core of the process is a group of people who will evaluate your request for funding, and your company, from the investor's perspective.

Red team members read your materials as if they were evaluating you for funding. This means that they will not be advocates for your company. Quite the opposite – if your presentation has serious problems or if they don't get what you're trying to say, it will more likely be, "This is not making sense as an investment!"

That in itself is more than a lot of VCs will do. They are in the business of finding opportunities and making investments – not critiquing your presentation. Many times all you will get is "Thanks for coming in – we will get back to you if we are interested." But a red team goes the extra step – it is in the business of helping you improve your chances of getting funded. In that role they play hardball; team members can be very critical, step on your toes if necessary, and pull no punches. A red team member who holds back honest and incisive criticism because of a fear of hurting someone's feelings is not helping the effort.

Red teaming can be a very unsettling experience for some founders – but the goal of each and every member of the team is to help improve the presentation, value proposition, business plan and chances of getting funded. Remember, to make a success you occasionally have to break a few egos!

Here are some guidelines we follow for forming and running a red team review:

- Because of their experience, members of our red teams emulate the process and mindset of the VCs that the company is going to present to.

- We pick at least three people to serve on each team.
- They are knowledgeable in the company's space.
- Team members must have no prior connection with the company that is presenting.
- They must be willing and able to commit the necessary time and attention to the process.
- We insist that members are given at least two days to read the materials to be used in the presentation and do a bit of personal research.
- Team members must be committed to helping the founders improve their chances of getting funded.

Benefits of a Red Team Review

Our independent review procedure emulates the investor community's initial-review decision making. We simulate first meetings with VCs and critically review the presentations. Our process delivers an in-depth, interactive debriefing of a funding request. The results will provide you with guidance and direction on what must be done to improve your probability of being funded.

Red team members read and research materials and discuss them among themselves prior to your actual presentation.

The team then sits through your presentation – a simulated initial meeting with a potential investor. The focus of the evaluation is on how well you presented your business plan, value proposition and answered the threshold questions that an investor is likely to ask.

Finally, the team delivers a thoroughly interactive debriefing. The focus is on specific recommendations for resolution of major issues. They also present recommendations and guidance on improvements relative to strengths, weaknesses, opportunities and threats.

Good Red-Teaming Programs

Good red teaming programs are designed to:

- Help founders become familiar with the process of red-teaming,
- Take them through a simulated initial meeting with a potential investor,
- Provide a critical review and assistance in refocusing and refining their presentation, and
- Guide them through the process of presenting to appropriate venture capitalists and private equity fund managers.

If you want to learn more about my red teaming programs and how they can help you improve your chances of getting funded, send me an e-mail and we will arrange a time for a free consultation.

Customers as Financiers

Customers can be one of your best, lower-cost sources of the financial resources essential to building your business – yet many early-stage companies totally ignore them.

~~~~~~~~~~~~~~~~~~~~

One of my suggested rules, 'If your product or service is as good as you think it is, and they want it badly enough, they will pay for developing it' … that your customers could supply the financing for your company's launch and early growth, drew a number of requests for a practical example. I'm going to devote this chapter to responding to those requests by describing the evolution of one of my own companies.

This one started, much like the others, because I had identified a major set of problems that a significant group of potential customers had. You will notice that I did not use the term 'market' … I have believed from the beginning that amateurs have 'markets' and pros have 'customers'. I began with potential customers and a series of face-to-face contacts with senior executives at those companies. I talked with them extensively, developed a solution to a set of challenges that they knew they had, presented that solution for review and then launched a company based on an agreed upon model.

In this case, the group of potential customers was the major US movie studios. Their challenge was the confluence of the rise of the independent film producers and the financial limits on their ability to produce and distribute films. The studios need to make and distribute as many films as possible in order to spread the risk. They do this to assure a higher probability that enough of them will be winners to pay for the 'dogs', the studio's overhead and generate a nice profit. The independent producers constituted an additional source of film projects. That was the good news. But there was an Ethiopian in the fuel supply.

In the late seventies the movie business was truly bicoastal. Production was centered on the west coast and mostly at the studio lots. Financing was provided by the money center banks, principally those in New York City ... where I was living at the time. The banks' position was that the credit lines of the studios were pretty much tapped out. Even though they recognized that producing and distributing more films would increase the chances of studio profits, they were uncomfortable significantly expanding the lines.

I had a number of friends in the 'business' that made me aware of the restrictions on the studios. I suppose, given my reputation for not being able to put down a complex problem until I'd come up with a viable solution, they conspired to prod me into going to work. Well, their strategy succeeded.

The problem was interesting, indeed challenging, as it involved two major industries with radically different cultures and perspectives on the world. The money center banks, although they had been providing financing to the film industry for decades, were mostly 'belts-and-suspenders' types who kept a very close eye on risk. The film industry was populated by significantly more entrepreneurial types who were willing to roll the dice ten times in order to win big two or three times. The two different cultures had been locked in a mutually beneficial relationship which was increasingly being stressed.

My first step was to get a thorough understanding of the problem and the dynamics of both perspectives. I talked to a wide range of bankers familiar with the industry and with senior executives in the film business. The principal result was that I now could see the world through the eyes of both the bankers and the studios … I could begin to craft a solution. A collateral result of this process was a partnership with a man who, at the time of our meeting, was CFO of Columbia Pictures.

My second step (and only after determining that there was a market for the solution we might develop) was to build a team of subject matter experts to take advantage of the knowledge I had gathered ... and to mount an assault on the challenge. We met over a period of several months and the group was expanded to include other skill sets. Each time we encountered a new area that needed to be covered I went on a search for the best in the field.

Finally we hit on a solution which would allow off balance sheet financing of the top twenty five percent of the risk chapter of each film project. Although the solution was complex, the underlying enabling conditions were quite simple. In those days the top marginal tax rate in New York City was somewhere around one hundred and three percent ... in other words, above a certain level of income, and if you lived in NYC, the combined governments would actually take more than you earned. But more broadly, the combined top marginal federal and state rates approached eighty to ninety percent.

So I involved some of the top tax lawyers in the City and we focused on refining the model. Working with the tax code made all the challenges more difficult as it involved not only tax lawyers but the Internal Revenue Service ... without their blessing the approach to the innovative financing would bear an unacceptable risk.

Well, to jump ahead a bit, we came up with

a solution that passed muster and presented it to both the studios and the banks. The banks loved it because they would now be able to spread their risk over a larger number of projects and be protected by taking the lower seventy five percent of the risk chapter. The studios were equally attracted to the idea because they could now finance and distribute a third more films. All that was needed at that point was a source of funds that would take the top twenty five percent of the risk in each project.

I had left Wall Street some two years earlier but had maintained a wide range of connections through the other businesses that I had started. One of my services was providing and vetting investment opportunities for the major clients of the front line street houses and what was then known as the 'big eight' … my how things have changed. Once the studios, the bank's and the IRS had signed off, I approached my clients. I presented my proposition. Because of a combination of tax and economic benefits, they and their major clients found the structure very appealing. The model was now complete.

So, after six months or so of hard and very detailed R&D, we were ready to launch the business. We had organized a source of product, a customer base and a source of financing. Beyond that our customer base had financed the R&D process … in other words; they were so interested in the development of a solution to their problem, and so attracted to the possibilities of our solution, that they provided the financing for the development process. The street houses, banks, studios and accounting firms all supported the R&D process because we were making sure that they all won big as a result. Rather than 'we-centric', we were 'you-centric'. We launched with several hundred thousand dollars' worth of no-cost R&D that was funded by the clients ... and we launched debt free into immediate profitability.

Fast forward to the late 90s. I had returned from doing my PhD work in Scotland. My wife and I decided to settle in the DC area. Here I could pursue my three principal interests ... business, politics and fishing. Imagine my surprise as I began to make contact with the 'bubble businesses'. Here was an entire industry based on the assumption that their clients were idiots who just didn't get the latest thing that these people were selling. I sat in on presentations where CEOs of equity funded science projects would rant about how stupid their clients were and how much easier life would be if they just left it all in the hands of 'Bleeding Edge, Inc.' The image of these pretentious people who never made a bottom line, talking openly derisively about people who regularly did, etched itself into my mind ... and, of course, into the minds of their never-to-be 'customers'.

Mercifully many of these people are now more appropriately placed as service providers in the fast food industry. The newer generation, along with the survivors of the bad old days, have a significantly different vision of the customer. Now the customer is most likely to be seen as the group of sharp people with a real business and real needs that, if effectively and creatively solved, could support an emerging business. Every now and then an entrepreneurial team will also discover potential customers as a source of R&D support and start-up funding. I highly recommend that experience. It sure beats throwing cold water on the fire that is supposed to warm your house.

Protecting Investor Interests - Quick Assessment, the Short List

I am sometimes asked by investors to 'parachute' into a company and give them a quick assessment of conditions and possibilities. Most of the time, the company has been under-performing. Frequently the money that the investors provided has been spent and they are facing the need for follow-on funding. The investors want to know if additional investment is prudent. Generally I am asked to opine on four options: 1) shut it down, 2) sell or merge the company, 3) overhaul the team and value proposition and re-launch, or 4) make an additional investment and stay the course. My first steps are to prioritize those options and present a quick summary of the strengths and weaknesses of each. I also focus on the threats and opportunities that will most likely present themselves.

I divide the assessment process into phases. The first phase is designed to surface early indicators that might either eliminate the need for further investigation or focus the effort along one or two of the options. Many times, the first phase can be completed within two to four weeks. A presentation of findings and recommendations can then be used by the investors to decide whether there is anything worth saving and to chart, at a high level, a strategy for moving forward. Occasionally the decision is to shut down the company. At others times it is to find another company to buy it. Less frequently, the way forward is to invest further funds. Most often the decision is made to sketch out an overhaul of the value proposition and management team in preparation for a re-launch. This latter option can require a short-term investment of cash to keep the doors open during the strategic review phase but may be the best way forward.

The approach is hierarchical. It seeks to eliminate options one at a time; starting with the first one. Sometimes things have gone so far down that the only option is to shut it down. If there is nothing worth saving or the cost of saving the company would be much higher than any expected return, there are few options. If the decision is made to close the doors, the assessment is over and the cleanup begins.

Most assessments reveal value that is worth protecting. As a result, the work continues. During this second phase, I use a seven-item screen to search for 'indicators'. These are conditions that, should they exist, generally mean that one or the other of the options is indicated.

Unwarranted Hubris: I know this might seem like a redundant title. Generally all hubris is seen as unwarranted. In fact, it is generally seen as a highly unattractive tendency in both individuals and companies. But there is some hubris that is worse than others; and that is a hubris that rests on having accomplished nothing at all. It is entirely pretense.

I remember a recent presentation at an angel investor conference. The presenting team was completely unaware that they were making fools of themselves. Investors would ask basic questions. The responses were always inadequate and poorly thought out. But the team soldiered on. Their mantra was "we are a bunch of smart guys and will figure that out when the need arises". Of course, most of the audience was thinking "if you are so damn smart, why didn't you realize that you would need to have effective answers to these basic questions ready?"

Another company was full of this 'change the world as we know it' crap. They saw themselves as missionaries converting the ignorant. I remember a presentation that they gave to potential follow-on investors. Their basic message was that their likely clients were behind the curve. (The company was still pre-revenue) They, the super-team, were on a mission to educate the masses and convert them to the new technology. When one of the potential investors pointed out that their 'ignorant likely clients' were running successful businesses that made profits and had solid balance sheets, the team responded that 'such success is no indication of anything'. The same realization was reached by every member of the audience at that very moment. The presentation was over even if the presenters did not realize it.

Sometimes this form of hubris is fueled by initial success or apparent success. A good example was one company that that developed a very innovative solution to a hard problem. That success generated a hubris that was magnificent to behold; if your stomach was strong enough. The problem came, of course, when the founders felt that monetization of their 'gift to the world' was far beneath them. Having spent the investors' money, they had proven how smart they were. They did manage to forget that the investors were in it for a return on their money. But then, as the CEO said, "investors are just money grubbers".

Hubris is a company killer. Once it sets in, it is very hard to eradicate. No logical conversation will help to mitigate the tendency. The habits of the management team will continue to destroy opportunities and increase costs. The behavior goes to branding and establishes the reputation of the company in the minds of potential customers. Arrogance is insulting and hubris is the worst kind of arrogance.

Too Much Talk and Not Enough Action: Business is all about monetizing the value proposition by getting customers to pay for the product or service. That is what investors really invest in. They want the team to turn concepts into revenue streams and manage expenses in such a way that profits are generated.

I am amazed at how many management teams fail to understand that seminal concept. Without customers, you do not have a company – you have a class project. I recently was asked to look at a company that had received and spent over ten million dollars from investors and were still pre-revenue. My initial interviews not only highlighted that fact but the underlying cause. Management understood that monetizing the value proposition was hard, would take a lot of work and would involve bringing all sorts of new skill sets onto the team. These were people that the management team referred to as foreigners. This meant dilution of their position and a short-term increase in the 'burn rate'. They preferred to collect their salaries, spend the investors' money and take the easy road. The problem came when the money ran out. The founders were convinced that the investors would put good money after bad to keep the doors open. They got two big shocks. First, doors closed and you're fired. Second, here's a lawsuit for negligence, fraud, misuse of funds and a bit more. The results, two personal bankruptcies with both founders now working as 'consultants'.

In a second company, the CEO was always

going on about how he had learned 'hard lessons' and how valuable that had been. His education had come at a very high cost. The investors' money had been spent and his company was on life support. Several people who had tried to help him were now creditors with little chance of getting paid. Employees were receiving subsistence-level, partial salary checks. All the talk about 'learning lessons' masked the fact that the team had not been able to effectively monetize the value propositions.

A team that is not spending ninety percent of its time implementing, monetizing the value proposition and generating revenue does not understand what being in business is all about. Without that clear understanding, the team is not worth investing in. Too much talk and not enough action is a recipe for loss of investment. The bare fact is that this lack is easy to diagnose.

Once a team has settled into an implementation avoidance pattern, it is very hard to change their behavior. Most of the time major surgery is required. In a number of cases, wholesale replacement of the senior team was the only viable solution. The central issue is the preservation and enhancement of shareholder value. When that is threatened, there is nothing to do but make the substantial changes or liquidate the company.

The Blind Leading the Blind: Knowing your competition is one of the core requirements of any successful business. It's not just about identifying potentially disruptive competition, (although that is very important) it means understanding what your competition is offering and how your company stacks up against those offerings. I am astounded at the levels of ignorance in some teams. The most extreme is the statement 'we don't really have any competition'. That is generally enough for me to shut down the assessment process and tell the investors that it is time to flush the toilet. Every company has competition and every value proposition does as well. Every company is competing for scarce resources, namely the customers' money, and that always has a variety of places to end up.

A variation of this ignorance is 'our competition is not nearly as good as we are'. I generally hear this from a CEO whose company is pre-revenue. He is almost always talking about a competing company that is turning a profit and has a history of success. His team is almost always pro-strategy and anti-implementation. And he is generally soon to be out of business and applying for a job at one of this 'inept competitors'. The measure of how good you and your team are is to be found in your customer base. The one definitive indicator that a company is offering a value proposition that has merit is that they have found a steadily growing group of customers who are willing to pay for it. You build that customer base by outperforming your competition. The company that consistently wins new customers is better than the one that does not.

A good example of the importance of this knowledge is to be found in the federal government contracting space. Government agencies and the major prime contractors are under a great deal of pressure – both budgetary and otherwise. The sales process is highly ritualized and heavily monitored. Priorities are shifting; partially because there is a new administration and also because of major trends in the economy. Subcontractors who make their living supporting primes need to be aware of these pressures and trends. As conditions change, the requirements of the agencies and prime contractors evolve. Failure to adjust understandings can make a company seem out of touch. As an old friend sued to say, "Do not attempt tomorrow's journeys using yesterday's maps".

The cost of not understanding your competition is very high. Management and the board need a thoroughgoing knowledge of the competitive space. They also need to understand the situations that their likely clients are facing. There is no substitute for that knowledge. Without it, it is literally the blind leading the blind.

A Culture of Entitlement: "We will get additional funding because we deserve it". I call this the 'little lord Fauntleroy' or 'little prince' syndrome. We all grow through phases and one of them has us feeling that our parents are going to take care of us and that, as their child, we are entitled to that care. Part of the journey to adulthood is the realization that relationships between adults are based on recognition of individual preferences and needs and a negotiated settlement that recognizes both. An attitude of entitlement is essentially a return to childhood and an ego-centric focus on one person's needs. In this case, it is the management team's focus on its own needs at the expense of the needs of the investors.

The most insidious implication of a culture of entitlement is that the investors' objectives are denigrated or ignored. Team members may give lip service but their actions consistently demonstrate that they have other, personal objectives that are higher priorities. The corrosive implication of such a culture is that the investors' interests will always be severely subordinated to the ego-driven interests of the management team. Once a culture of entitlement settles in, it is almost impossible to change without wholesale replacements within the senior team.

Waste a Lot Have Not: Initially I comb through the income statements of a company. It is amazing how much you can learn by studying patterns of expenditures. The casual assumptions of what is appropriate or necessary to maintain the 'image of the company' gives you insight into how the senior team is viewing the question of conservation of resources. Some of these priorities are easily observed. In one case, the team bought each member a new laptop even though they were replacing serviceable ones. The same team purchased top-of-the-line cell phones with the most expensive service plans. When asked whether these expenditures would deliver a good return on the investment, the CEO responded as if the question was pure gibberish.

There is a lot of debate over what makes a successful entrepreneur but I suspect that there is one characteristic on which there is almost unanimous agreement. Good entrepreneurs make a dollar go farther and get more value out of it. They don't turn one loose unless they have to and they don't fritter away funds. I like to work with CEOs who are justifiably proud of how far they can stretch investors' funds. Maybe it is the Scot in me, but I feel that such an attitude is one of the seminal indicators of pending success.

Good entrepreneurs hate the very idea of 'burn rate' while poor ones take pride in high burn rates. The attitude towards this concept is a handy indicator when you are trying to separate out the business builders from the venture-backed consultants. The most effective way to attack a burn rate is to generate revenues. Lack of revenues is generally a sign of a very dangerous dynamic; a management team that has neither the drive nor the ability to monetize the value proposition.

~~~~~~~~~~~~~~~~~~~~~

The last two areas in my initial screen touch on the relationship between management and the investors. They are ticklish topics because they open the possibility that the behavior of the investors has been contributing to, and even supporting, the failure of the management team. Needless to say, I approach both of them very gingerly.

Performance Metrics: I begin looking for performance metrics from the start and always take their absence as a big red flag. The investors have provided funds to the company and metrics are the codification of their expectations. The initial charge may vary from 'go forth and do great things' to 'here is the basis that you will earn-in to the company'. The first is an indication that investors have made a grant to the company. The second shows that the investors see the company as worth the total of funds invested until the management team adds value. There are, of course, lots of variations within these two extremes. But my initial screen is designed to determine whether there are any effective performance metrics in play.

To be very clear on this, the lack of effective performance metrics is an indictment of the investors' approach to investing. Most management teams will prefer to operate without them if that is an option. Most would prefer to get their carried interest in the company with having to earn-in. I say most because the very best entrepreneurs insist on performance metrics and they are willing to tie their interest in the company to how well they perform.

When asked what the proper valuation of a start-up company, I always respond 'the total investment in the company plus a small percentage for the management team'. This formulation is often a conversation stopper with both entrepreneurs and investors. I go one to explain that the best way to approach an investment in start-up and middle market companies is to deploy and enforce performance metrics that allow the team to earn-in. The formulas used should allow them to accumulate a very large percentage ownership in the company. Indeed, there are levels of performance that would make the investors very happy to end up with a minority interest. The question is how closely performance is tied to attainment of these results.

Performance metrics define the relationship and understanding between investors and the management team. The lack of metrics means there is no understanding; no matter what any other agreements say. Thoroughgoing metrics indicate a clear and well-defined understanding.

Governance, Oversight and Reporting: One of the most ignored corporate functions, particularly in start-ups, is governance. Oversight is the mechanism that investors use to keep track of the company's performance and challenges. The lack of an effective board of directors and oversight is a condition that I frequently encounter. Investors attempt to engage in oversight through a range of alternative strategies, but none are as effective as a well-run and populated board of directors.

Governance and oversight are actually a far more complex and subtle issues than it might initially seem. All investors rightfully insist on being involved in their portfolio companies. The real question is how and how much involvement. There are a number of approaches that I look for. All of them can have negative impacts on the company.

The Shadow CEO: This situation occurs mostly in start-up and middle-market, privately held companies and with investors who have had some success in their own right. An angel investor might insist on micro-managing the CEO of the company. The result is a form of castration. The CEO does not have the ability or authority to fill the leadership role. The team quickly realizes that the real power behind the throne is the investor. As a result, the team is dysfunctional and results suffer. Companies run in this way seldom prosper.

My Way or the Highway: I know one investor who reduces all of his investments to spreadsheets. He insists on detailed analysis and grumbles when the CEO or CFO does not know how to create complex spreadsheets. As a result, all of his portfolio companies suffer. There is little recognition that business is, first and foremost, about the team and teams are all about team members. The investor has a strong anti-humanist personality. Interpersonal issues are ignored and the teams tend to disintegrate. Another investor has a strong focus on product development but little patience for marketing and sales. This is mostly because her background is in the technology that allowed her to build a company and sell it out for a fat profit. But, as an investor, she confronts every challenge as if it was twenty years ago when conditions allowed such blind spots.

The Crazy, Rich Uncle: Another investor takes a 'kindly uncle' approach to 'helping the kid get started in business'. Oversight tends to be a series of 'firm conversations' followed by another check. The investor, who built a couple of businesses and sold them, talks in terms of those businesses in their mature state. The lessons he delivers do not relate to the challenges that the CEO is facing. Lacking professional oversight, the CEO tends to tolerate the crazy uncle's tendency to tell irrelevant stories as long as the checks keep coming.

When asked by investors about the best way to build a board for their companies, I always deliver the same message. "You stay off the board. Let's find three potential board members who understand the space the company is operating in and let them provide oversight. They will report to you as shareholders".

Protecting Investor Interests: Good governance is the key to enforcing performance metrics. Enforced performance metrics are the best way to avoid the problems discussed above. Protecting investors' interest involves putting both in place.

From my experience, there is value worth saving in most portfolio companies. Some will not survive as a free-standing company. They will need to be merged into another, larger and more professionally run operation. Others will need major surgery. This is particularly true in cases where the core of the value proposition is very good but the management team is not the one to monetize it. I find this regularly in companies that have made strides in the past but are now stuck on a revenue plateau. The old saying 'the people who got you here are not the ones who will take you to the next level' is often relevant. It is rare that I recommend follow-on investment without alteration of the performance metrics and governance approach. Additional investment is a serious step and should be approached as an opportunity to 'tighten up' the understanding between investors and the management team.

In the advisory business there are lots of consultants who work with management teams. Their advocacy supports the team's agenda. But there are few who operate as I do. I stand to protect the interests of the investors.

An Alternative to the Money Chase

Driving a Broken Wheel

One of the most frustrating things about getting a business off the ground, up and running, is the money chase. There seems to be no end to the meetings without tangible results or the polite 'don't call us, we'll call you' responses to a polished and passionate presentation. I regularly encounter founders who are at the end of their rope and absolutely certain that potential investors have simply been toying with them in some perverse game of cat and mouse. Their teams are disintegrating, creditors are knocking then pounding on the door and the future looks bleaker each day. Worse, the time spent in the money chase has bled effort and resources away from building out the team and refining the business plan. It is sad that this is such a frequently occurring experience. It is even sadder that it does not have to be that way at all.

It is widely accepted that the current model for venture capital and private equity investment is broken. Investors, who provide funding, are increasingly intrusive and, at times, overbearing. One recently told me that "we like to be in control of our destiny". My response was to ask, "does that mean that the founders have to give up control of theirs?" The question was clearly seen as irrelevant and an inconvenience.

These investors operate more as shadow CEOs. Founders and their teams become their captives. Their business instincts and understanding of their space become subordinated to the 'one-size-fits-all', soft Machiavellian vision of the investors. It's past time to find an alternative.

Shallow Focus Yields Shallow Results

One of the reasons that the model is broken is that institutional investors have ceded the final investment decisions to a group of fund managers who have insisted on a process that suits them but does not serve the process well. The first weakness is an insistence on an 'elevator speech". Investors prowl the networking events listing to one thirty-second pitch after another as if they were using a metal detector and listening for the squeal of a find.

A second weakness is the preference that presentations be in the form of a PowerPoint slide deck. If elevator speeches are the poster children for shallow thinking, slide decks are the very definition if it. A mentor was fond of telling me "if you can sum it up in 30 seconds or a set of bullets, it is either not worth your time or you don't understand what you are talking about. If the people you are talking to either demand or assume that you can do that, they are not worth talking to." Personally, I prefer conversations that start off "it's complicated"; followed by evidence of a sophisticated grasp of difficult and complex issues. That conversation is worth my time – speed dating is not.

Founders would do better with an approach that allows their team to focus on building out the plan, sharpening the value propositions, developing customers and refining the financial model. Time spent in the money chase does not advance the value of the company nor does it increase the probability that it will succeed and flourish. A different approach is needed; one that significantly improves the viability of new companies by reducing the unproductive burdens on the team.

Shifting the Focus – Resetting the Priorities – Distributing the Burden

One new approach is offered by Growthers. Growthers maintains relationships with a range of funding sources. Our strength is in matching the investment objectives of those sources with the teams we are working with. For the most part, these are directly with the sources of investment. This disintermediation allows us to assume the burdens associated with arranging funding and frees the teams we incubate to focus on building their businesses. We organize and streamline the money chase and then manage it. In addition to streamlining the funding process and relieving your team of its burden, we bring a number of other benefits to the teams I work with:

- We allow you to focus on building your team and the business:
- You get relief from the senseless and time wasting grind of the money chase
- Ours is a process that is designed, from start to finish, to meet the investment criteria of our investor partners
- We provide support for building out your team and developing and testing your business plan
- Growthers provides governance and oversight on behalf of the investors post-investment
- We support teams that are interested in growing by further acquisition
- You receive ongoing strategic advisory from high-level individuals and companies

The net result is that:

- you have a greater chance of actually getting funded
- on terms that are competitive with those that the venture funds offer
- will spend much more time developing your business and customers
- will not have to suffer the intrusiveness of the typical VC oversight

- can focus on building your business rather than setting off on the money chase

Parting Thoughts

In the heat of the money chase it is easy to lose track of the fact that the process involves bringing two distinct world views into agreeable focus. Investors are in business to make investments in companies that will have a high probability of yielding a substantial return. They are seeking opportunities that will pay off within their planning horizon by either cashing them out or resulting in a substantially increased valuation.

Management, on the other hand, is in the business of building a company. Their horizon stretches much farther out. They are also involved in the much more complicated process of building a company.

If the money chase is going to end satisfactorily for both, it is necessary that both sides honor and accept the objectives of the other. Adversarial tendencies have no productive role in this process. Neither does the denigration of one side by the other.

In the chapters above, I have tried to highlight some of the blind alleys and unproductive approaches that can so easily pollute this process. It is far too easy to spend massive amounts of time and treasure pursuing a path that will end up costing both sides and benefiting neither.

The hard truth is that there is more money available than there are investment grade deals. Investors are constantly on the hunt for companies to invest in. If you want to get funded you need to inhabit the mindset of these investors and understand the criteria that drives their process. The same unproductive approach, pursued over and over, will not get you funded. If what you are doing is not helping you reach that goal, you need to rethink your approach and deepen your understanding of the 'rules of the game'.

I've had years of experience - both with my own companies and with those of others. Let me help you turn the corner and reach your objective.

Contact Information

I sincerely hope that you have enjoyed this book and find it useful. I am always interested to hear from readers—about their thoughts on the book or relevant war stories that relate to it. Please feel free to send either to drsmith@dr-smith.com.

If you are interested in exploring the possibility of building a business development team and/or an advisory board for your company, send me an e-mail. Provide me with as much information as you can. I will contact you to arrange a free consultation.

Dr. Earl R. Smith II
Washington DC
June 2014

DrSmith@Dr-Smith.com